EDUCATION AND DEMOCRACY IN AN AGE OF ENCOUNTER

ADAM F STROM

EDUCATION AND DEMOCRACY IN AN AGE OF ENCOUNTER

Education and Democracy in an Age of Encounter: What Schools Must Do Now

Published by Encounter Press
An imprint of Re-Imagining Migration
Boston, Massachusetts
reimaginingmigration.org

ISBN: 979-8-9958398-0-4
Printed in the United States of America
First Edition, 2026

DEDICATION

For Margot and Terry, who taught me first.
For Max and Sam, who teach the rising generation.
For Sandy, who teaches me still.
For all the amazing educators, visionaries, colleagues
— and those I wish were colleagues—
who teach me every single day.

CONTENTS

ACKNOWLEDGEMENTS

Books are built from conversations, and this one more than most. The members of the Re-Imagining Migration team are the most extraordinary thought partners I could imagine. Meisha Lamb-Bell, Jessica Lander, Sara K. Ahmed, Sara Hunaidi, and Karel Karpe bring to this work a combination of intellectual rigor, moral seriousness, and genuine joy that I did not know was possible in a single organization. Everything in this book has been tested against what they know and what they do. They are special people and even more remarkable as a team.

The teachers who have let me into their classrooms, their professional development sessions, their doubts and their breakthroughs — you are the proof of the argument. Every claim this book makes about what is possible rests on what I have watched you do. Your students and our communities will be better because of what you do.

Martha Minow read an early draft with the kind of attention that only a scholar who cares about the argument can bring. Her critique was generous, precise, and made the book better in ways I am still discovering. Scott Gold, a long-time friend and a veteran teacher, asked to read the last draft of the book, and while I was terrified sharing it with him, he gave me extraordinary feedback that helped refine my thinking.

While not involved in the book, I deeply value conversations I have had over the years with Anthony Appiah, Carol Gilligan, Carola Suárez-Orozco, Marcelo Suárez-Orozco, Verónica Boix Mansilla, Dimity Anselme (who had the misfortune of sharing an office with me), and so many other scholars and educators whose work has shaped how I think about migration, identity, and education. I am grateful for years of conversation and collaboration.

Sandy Smith-Garcés is my wife and my most patient audience. She has heard almost every idea in this book — usually delivered as an interruption while she is trying to read the morning paper or draft tours for K–12 students, university groups, and the general public at the Museum of Fine Arts in Boston. That she has remained both brilliant and kind throughout this process is a testament to qualities I can admire but not fully explain.

PROLOGUE

This book began as a screed and then an essay. Then it became several essays. By the time I understood it had become a book, the urgency was already clear. This could not wait.

We are living through a moment in which the questions this book addresses — about belonging, about difference, about what education owes to a pluralistic democracy — are being contested in real time, in school boards, legislatures, courtrooms, and classrooms. I felt an obligation to contribute whatever I could to that conversation, and to do so now.

I have spent thirty years working at the intersection of research and practice, of memory and argument, of the classroom and the archive. This book reflects that. It does not always speak in a single register because my career has not unfolded in one. Some of what follows is philosophy, some is memoir, some is something closer to field reporting. I have not tried to resolve that into a single voice, because the argument needs each of these voices, and each of these traditions, to converge on the most urgent educational and civic challenge of our time.

This book was not written to sit on a shelf. It was written to be used — by educators, by parents, by anyone who believes that how we prepare young people to live with one another cannot wait.

INTRODUCTION

"I learned it is possible to pray at night and ride in a Jim Crow car the next morning and to feel comfortable doing both. I learned to believe in freedom, to glow when the word democracy was used, and to practice slavery from morning to night."
Lillian Smith, Killers of the Dream

My mother grew up in Memphis, Tennessee, in a world organized around a lie. The lie was that some people were fundamentally different from others — different in capacity, in worth, in their claim to full humanity. That lie was encoded in law, enforced by violence, and maintained by the everyday rituals of ordinary life: separate water fountains at the department store, separate waiting rooms at the Greyhound station.

Her school sat directly across the street from the Memphis Zoo. From her classroom window, she saw the entrance signs indicating that "coloreds" were allowed to enter only on Thursdays.

Inside, she learned about American democracy in civics class. The ideal of democracy was on the lesson board; the reality of segregation was just outside the window. She received both at the same time, yet school offered no help reconciling these contradictions. The hypocrisy was visible every day, yet it went unmentioned.

She went to school. She learned to read and write. She learned arithmetic and history — a particular kind of history, taught in a particular way. The Civil War was called the War Between the States. She was taught how the South won the major battles. In her Tennessee history class, she did not learn who lost the Civil War. "Bad history" was best forgotten.

There was a powerful silence about race and racism. No mention of antisemitism or the Holocaust — and she was a Jewish girl in the Jim Crow South, which placed her squarely on the line between inclusion and exclusion. The silence covered everything that mattered most. While she graduated from high school and college and later earned a master's degree, her education did not help her understand the world she lived in.

Years later, my sister showed her an excerpt from Lillian Smith's memoir Killers of the Dream, which she felt put words to her own experience.

"The silence was the curriculum. In many ways, it still is."

And yet: the faces my mother saw as a child, the faces of love and care, were Black women and Black men. Her parents worked full-time, and there was always someone in the house — caretakers who raised her alongside her mother and father. She loved them, and they loved her. And every bit of her public life was organized to deny the humanity of those very people. To the day she died, her memories of the indignities her caretakers and friends suffered shamed her and brought her to tears. Her school had no language for this.

School offered no help in making sense of a community where the people who cared for you were barred from the zoo, except one day a week, where tenderness and injustice were both in the air she breathed, and in a neighborhood where a child could be taught compassion and complicity in the same breath.

Her real education, she would later write, was family-centered. Her parents taught her the meaning of social justice, the importance of political participation, and standing up for the underdog because, as a Jew, she was an underdog too. But this was despite her schooling, not because of it. The institution charged with preparing her to understand her world had nothing to say about the world she actually lived in.

* * *

I have thought about this often in the decades since, as I have devoted my professional life to the question of what education might accomplish if it took its responsibility to prepare young people for the world they actually inhabit seriously. What I have come to believe is this: my mother's education was not a failure unique to its time and place. It was an extreme instance of a failure that persists — a failure of purpose, a retreat from the hardest and most essential questions education might address.

We live now in a different world from the one my mother navigated. The formal structures of American apartheid have been dismantled. But we still live in a world organized around encounters with difference — encounters that schools largely leave young people to navigate on their own. We are more connected across lines of culture and geography than any generation in human history, and yet people are often bewildered, threatened, or enraged by what we find on the other side of those connections.

Encounters with the other are not rare or unusual. It is the permanent fact of the human experience. In our time, demographic transformation is changing communities across the developed world. According to the 2020 United States Census, there is a 61.1% chance that when two random people meet, they will be from different racial and ethnic groups.

Why? Migration — chosen and forced — continues to reweave the human fabric. Digital technologies collapse the distances that once separated people with different backgrounds and experiences. The question is not whether our children will encounter difference, but whether they will be prepared to engage it with understanding rather than fear, with curiosity rather than contempt.

The questions that have organized my career, and that organize this book, are: Which institution is positioned to prepare young people for this world at scale? Which institution touches nearly every child, across lines of class, culture, and geography? Which institution has the time, the authority, and the mandate to undertake this work systematically?

The answer, of course, is schools.

And yet schools have largely retreated from this responsibility. Over the past half-century, American education has progressively narrowed its civic purpose, and the narrowing has been driven not only by educators but by the policymakers and philanthropists who shape what schools are asked to do and how they are judged for doing it.

We have moved from a textbook industry to a testing industry to one now enamored with artificial intelligence — each transition promising transformation, each delivering a more sophisticated apparatus for measuring and delivering the wrong things. The technical has crowded out the moral and ethical. The measurable too often displaces the meaningful, and we have reduced civic education to a subject called "civics," confined ethics to the margins, and treated the capacities required to navigate pluralism as someone else's problem.

This is not a call to return to some golden age. There is no golden age to return to. The history of American public education is more complicated than that — a story of liberation and oppression intertwined, of genuine aspiration and systematic betrayal.

That history is the subject of the next chapter, because any call to reclaim education's civic purpose must reckon with the fact that "civic purpose" has too often meant the imposition of one group's vision on everyone else.

But the research on what makes encounters with difference productive — what conditions allow human beings to navigate difference with understanding rather than fear — offers genuine hope. This is not simply optimism about human nature, but grounded evidence of what becomes possible when the right conditions are created. That research, and what it reveals about the role schools might play, is the subject of the chapters that follow.

I come to this argument not as a theorist but as someone who has spent more than thirty years trying to make it work in practice. My mother founded Facing History and Ourselves on a premise that sounds simple and is not: that studying the worst of human behavior might illuminate the best of human possibility. I spent twenty-two years there helping build curricula, train teachers, and document what happened when young people were given the tools to grapple seriously with history's hardest questions. I saw what became possible. I also saw what remained beyond our reach.

Eight years ago, I co-founded Re-Imagining Migration, an organization dedicated to transforming how schools prepare young people for lives shaped by human movement and encounter. I have watched educators across the country attempt this work, often against great resistance and with inadequate support. I have seen what succeeds and what fails, what research supports and what remains to be proven.

This book is not a manual for that organization's approach. It is a broader argument — one that I hope will be taken up by people who will never encounter Re-Imagining Migration, who will develop their own programs and practices, and who will create solutions beyond what any of us has yet imagined. The scale of the challenge requires a movement, not a brand. It requires a shared sense of purpose that transcends institutions and ideologies.

What I offer here is a beginning: a synthesis of what research reveals, a framework for thinking about what education might accomplish, and an invitation to join a conversation that is only starting. The conversation is urgent because the conditions that make it necessary are accelerating, and because the consequences of inaction are already visible amid the polarization, fear, and democratic fragility that mark our current moment.

My mother eventually found her way to an education that helped her understand the world she had grown up in. It was not the education her schools provided. She had to build it herself, over decades, through reading, conversation, and the slow, painful work of making sense.

She should not have had to build it herself. That is what schools are for.

This book is about what it would mean to take that responsibility seriously as the animating purpose of education in an age of encounter.

PART I

The Conditions

THE ENCOUNTER IS THE CONDITION

Note to the reader: This chapter contains slurs that were used against a classmate. I have included them because sanitizing the language would sanitize the experience – and the point of this book is that we cannot look away from what happens when schools fail to build the conditions that young people deserve.

"The question is not whether our children will encounter difference, but whether they will be prepared to navigate it with understanding rather than fear, with curiosity rather than contempt."

On my subway ride to work every morning, the world is sitting in the seats, holding the bars. Most people are quiet, lost in their phones or their thoughts. But I hear English, Spanish, and Chinese every day — sometimes Portuguese, sometimes Haitian Creole, sometimes languages I cannot identify. When I'm crammed close to other passengers, I see them watching videos from India, Haiti, and the Middle East. There are Jews, Catholics, Protestants, Muslims, Hindus, and probably many more that I cannot instantly recognize — or am afraid to guess. The train car is more of a microcosm of human diversity than anyone who rode this same line fifty years ago would believe.

This is the encounter that demographic change is making unavoidable — and that I have seen not as a challenge to be managed but as one of the great sources of energy and revitalization in our communities. The languages I hear on that train, the foods that have transformed my neighborhood, the ideas and ways of seeing the world that colleagues and neighbors and students have brought into my life — these are gifts, not disruptions. Not everyone experiences it that way. For some, the same changes feel disorienting, even threatening — a world becoming unfamiliar faster than they can make sense of it. Both responses are real. What determines which one prevails is not the encounter itself, but the conditions under which it happens — and whether anyone has prepared us to meet it. That is what education is for. And that is what it has largely failed to do.

In the Boston of the 1970s, the city was 80 percent white. Latinos made up less than 3 percent of the population — fewer than 67,000 in all of Massachusetts. In my neighborhood and my school, the number was essentially zero. I had one Cuban friend in elementary school. He was a group of one — the only Latino kid in the neighborhood.

Anti-Black violence scarred the city during the busing crisis; I watched it on the news and heard it in the conversations around me. I had a Black friend whose house was attacked by kids in the neighborhood. That house is around the corner from where I am writing. We knew it happened. None of us talked about it much.

Definitely not at school. The school had no language for what was happening in the streets around it, no curriculum that might help us make sense of the hatred we were witnessing, no adults who seemed to think this was something young people needed to understand.

In 1979, Iranian refugees began taking their seats in the schools I attended in Brookline. After the revolution and the hostage crisis, Persian families fleeing Iran began showing up in the Boston suburbs. But in the atmosphere of 1979 and 1980, with the nightly news counting the days of American captivity, with yellow ribbons on every tree, they became targets. In Cleveland Circle, not far from where I lived, an Iranian student named Majidi was killed by local teenagers. I don't remember anyone talking about it at school. I don't remember any assembly, any moment of reckoning, any teacher helping us understand what had happened or why.

What I do remember is a Persian kid at my high school who was brutally taunted. Towel head. Camel jockey. He was also called a faggot — one form of othering piled onto another. I once saw him surrounded by bullies in the bathroom, backed against the wall.

The school had no language for any of it — no curriculum that connected what was happening in Tehran to what was happening in our hallways, no adults who helped us understand that the kid being shoved against the tiles had fled the same regime we were taught to hate. He was Iranian. That was enough.

* * *

Consider the world a child born today will navigate.

By the time she enters kindergarten, the majority of American children under five will be from communities that were, within living memory, called "minorities." By the time she graduates high school, the nation will have no racial majority at all. The town she grew up in may look nothing like the town her grandparents knew. The neighborhood may have transformed in a single generation — new languages on the street signs, new foods in the grocery stores, new holidays observed, new ways of being in the world made suddenly visible.

Or perhaps she lives in a community that has changed very little, where the faces, names, and customs remain as they have been for generations. Even there, she will not be insulated. The world will come to her via screens, through the movement of people and goods and ideas, through the unavoidable fact that the boundaries that once separated communities have become permeable in ways they have never been before.

She will work alongside people whose backgrounds differ from hers. She will encounter, daily, perspectives shaped by experiences she has never had. She will be asked to make sense of conflicts rooted in histories she was never taught. She will vote on questions that require her to weigh the interests of people she will never meet, in places she will never visit, whose lives are nonetheless bound up with her own.

This is not a prediction about some distant future. It is a description of the present.

* * *

The United States is in the midst of a demographic transformation more profound than any since the great waves of immigration a century ago — and in some ways more profound than that. Between 1970 and today, the foreign-born population of the United States has more than quadrupled, from under ten million to over forty-five million. One in four children in American schools has at least one immigrant parent. In the largest school districts, that number approaches one in two.

The Census Bureau now calculates something called a "Diversity Index" — the probability that two people chosen at random will be from different racial or ethnic groups. In 2010, that probability was about 55 percent. By 2020, it had risen to over 61 percent. Among children under eighteen, it is nearly 70 percent. The younger the population, the more diverse it is — which means the future is already here, sitting in our classrooms, waiting to see whether we will prepare them for the world they will inherit.

But immigration is only part of the story. Internal migration is reshaping the country — rural to urban, urban to suburban, Rust Belt to Sun Belt, and now, increasingly, back again. Climate change is beginning to move people in ways we are only starting to understand, as drought, flood, and fire make some places uninhabitable and others suddenly desirable. The pandemic accelerated patterns of remote work that have untethered employment from geography, scrambling the demographics of communities that had been stable for decades.

The result is that fewer Americans live in places that look like they did a generation ago. The all-white small town, the ethnically defined urban neighborhood, and the suburb, sorted by race and religion, have been interrupted by economics and opportunity. With historical hindsight, we might recognize that migration is the throughline of the story of North America.

This is not uniquely American. Across the developed world, migration and demographic change are remaking societies. Germany, which long insisted it was not a country of immigration, now has a foreign-born population larger in proportion than the United States. The United Kingdom voted to leave the European Union in large part over anxieties about migration — and then discovered that immigration continued anyway, just from different places. France, Italy, Spain, the Netherlands, Sweden — every major European nation is contending with questions of identity, belonging, and difference that would have seemed abstract a generation ago.

* * *

And then there are the screens.

A child born today will grow up with access to more information, more perspectives, more voices than any human being in history. She will be able to watch events unfold in real time on the other side of the planet. She will encounter ideas, arguments, and ways of life that her grandparents could have gone a lifetime without ever confronting. She will form relationships — friendships, even — with people she has never met in person, people who live in different countries, speak different languages, inhabit different cultural worlds.

But liberation is not the whole story. The same technologies that connect us across difference also allow us to sort ourselves into enclaves of the like-minded, to construct information environments that confirm what we already believe, to encounter difference only in the form of outrage and conflict. The algorithms that govern what we see are optimized for engagement, and engagement is most reliably produced by content that provokes strong emotion, often framing difference as threat.

And the collapse is not only emotional but epistemic. A child today encounters information lacking any reliable way to distinguish journalism from opinion, reporting from propaganda, fact from fabrication. The skills required to make sense of this environment — to evaluate sources, to recognize manipulation, to hold provisional beliefs while keeping open to evidence — these are not innate. They must be taught.

* * *

Despite far-right calls for "remigration," the encounter with difference is not going away. It cannot be wished away, legislated away, or walled away. The forces driving demographic change and global connection are too powerful to be reversed by any policy or politics.

It's important to recognize that the change that comes with migration is disorienting. Those changes are experienced by those on the move and the communities where newcomers settle.

Often we focus on the impact of those changes on newcomers, but it is worth recognizing that communities transform with migration as well. I'd argue that the long term impact of those changes are often for the better, but it's important to note that for many people, change equals loss and the loss is real. The community that existed a generation ago, whatever its limitations, was a community, and its passing deserves to be mourned even as we acknowledge the injustices that were so often built into it. To dismiss the anxieties that attend demographic transformation as mere bigotry is to misunderstand both the nature of the anxiety and the nature of bigotry. People can be genuinely unsettled by change without being hateful. They can find it hard to adapt without being enemies of adaptation. And yet that same disorientation is exactly what demagogues exploit — stoking racism, antisemitism, Islamophobia, and xenophobia to harvest grievance rather than address it.

But the promise to reverse the change is a lie. It cannot be delivered. The migration has already happened. The children have already been born. The connections have already been made. The question is not whether we will live in a world of encounter, but how we will navigate the encounters we cannot avoid.

And here the research is unambiguous: how we negotiate these encounters is not determined by the encounters themselves. Proximity to difference can produce understanding or suspicion, cooperation or conflict, integration or fragmentation. The outcome depends on conditions — conditions that can be shaped, designed, and constructed. Left to chance, the encounter may go badly. Treated with intention, it can go well.

This is where education enters the story.

THE DREAM AND ITS BETRAYAL

"You can belong, but only if you stop being who you are."

Before the betrayal, the dream. When the Civil War ended, four million people rose from slavery with demands that were as immediate as they were profound — for land, for wages, for the reunification of families that had been torn apart, for legal recognition of their humanity. Among the most urgent was the demand for schools.

The Freedman's Bureau helped create more than 4,000 schools in five years. But the Bureau didn't create the hunger that preceded any government program. Booker T. Washington described it: "It was a whole race trying to go to school. Few were too young, and none too old, to make the attempt to learn." Charlotte Forten, a Black teacher from Philadelphia who went south to teach on the Sea Islands of South Carolina, wrote in her diary: "I never before saw children so eager to learn."

This was not an institutional, top-down initiative. It was people who had been denied literacy seizing it as the instrument of their own liberation.

Frederick Douglass had understood this decades earlier. Learning to read, he wrote, was "the pathway from slavery to freedom." His enslaver had understood it too, which is why teaching enslaved people to read was illegal in most Southern states. The prohibition itself was an indication of what slaveholders knew: literacy was not a skill; it was a threat. A person who could read could question. A person who could question was a threat to the very worldview that was used to justify slavery.

This is the liberatory tradition — the oldest and most radical strain in American education. Before there was a common school, before there was a Department of Education, before there was any system at all, people who had been told they were property insisted on their humanity and reached for books as the instrument of that insistence. The dream was liberation. The dream was real.

* * *

Horace Mann had a different dream — related, but fatally compromised.

Mann believed that common schools could solve America's deepest problems. If children from all backgrounds sat together in the same classrooms, they would grow into citizens capable of democratic self-governance. Education would be "the great equalizer of the conditions of men." The aspiration was genuine. And the aspiration contained a poison.

The common school's version of "all backgrounds" had terms. The terms were set by those who already held power — white, Protestant, English-speaking. The King James Bible was read in classrooms. Catholic families objected and were told the Bible was nonsectarian — a claim that only someone blinded by power could make with a straight face. Jewish children sat through Christian prayers. Indigenous children were removed from their communities entirely. The languages immigrants spoke at home were treated as obstacles to be overcome, rather than as resources to be honored. Everyone could enter the common school. But the price of entry was assimilation on someone else's terms.

The project was not a good goal pursued through bad means. The goal itself was the problem. Learning to live together, as Mann conceived it, meant becoming the same. And the sameness was never neutral. It was a particular cultural formation masquerading as the universal.

The violence of this was not always metaphorical. Captain Richard Henry Pratt, founder of the Carlisle Indian Industrial School, stated the logic plainly in 1892: the goal was to "kill the Indian in him, and save the man." Over the following decades, the federal government established or funded more than 400 boarding schools for Native children. Children as young as four were removed from families. Their names were taken. Their languages were forbidden. They were punished — physically, sometimes sexually — for the crime of being who they were. The Interior Department's 2022 investigation found marked and unmarked graves at more than fifty school sites across the country.

This was not an aberration from the American educational project. This was the American educational project, applied with explicit rather than implicit violence. Pratt and Mann shared a fundamental assumption: difference was a problem to be solved.

* * *

But the common school was not the only educational tradition in America. It was the dominant one — the one with state power behind it. Alongside it, sometimes hidden, sometimes tolerated, sometimes actively suppressed, communities built their own.

Black Americans built schools out of necessity and conviction — education as liberation, not assimilation, rooted in a community's own understanding of what freedom required. The Catholic school movement — driven initially by Irish immigrants, later joined by Italians, Poles, and others — arose in direct response to the Protestant character of the common school. Jewish communities established supplementary schools — not because we were excluded from public education, but because we understood that public education would not transmit what we needed to remain who we were.

What these traditions share is an understanding the common school refused: that a community's survival depends on transmitting more than skills. Identity, heritage, language, and faith are not obstacles to civic participation. They are the ground from which participation becomes meaningful.

John Dewey was asking a different question. He wanted to know what democracy required of education — not of any particular community, but of the institution itself. His answer was that democracy was not primarily a system of government but a way of living together, a set of habits and capacities that had to be cultivated, not assumed. The school was where that cultivation happened.

I should be transparent about something. This entire book was inspired by Dewey's *Democracy and Education*. When I first read it, it lit me up. The title of this book is a deliberate echo of his — a way of acknowledging what I owe him and what I am still trying to work out.

But Dewey's universalism came from somewhere. His image of the child learning through experience, of the school as a democratic community in miniature, was drawn from a particular experience — privileged, unmarked, presenting itself as simply human.

Dewey believed schools could be laboratories of democracy, and he was right. But his vision carried a hidden assumption: that the students entering those laboratories were roughly interchangeable, that difference was a temporary condition on the way to a common identity. He did not reckon seriously with what it meant to build democratic community across lines of race, language, and culture that were never going to dissolve, nor with whose experience would be treated as the default, and whose would need to assimilate to it.

In that sense, he was Mann's heir as much as his critic. The coercion was gone. The assumption of universality remained.

I want to take his core insight further than he did. If democracy is a mode of associated living, the obligation to prepare young people for encounters with difference belongs to every institution that shapes the young — in classrooms and after-school programs, in community organizations and houses of worship, in all the spaces where adults form what children come to believe about themselves and about others. The research and examples I draw on come mostly from public schools, because that is where the evidence is richest and the civic argument most explicitly made. But the responsibility I am describing stops at no institution's door.

We will return to Dewey in a few chapters. Scholars who have carried his tradition forward with clear eyes — people like John Rogers at UCLA, whose work on youth civic engagement I admire deeply — are among the education thinkers I find most essential. His vision demands our attention. The critique is not the last word.

James Baldwin was asking the same question in 1963, from a position Dewey never occupied. Speaking to New York educators in October of that year — weeks after the March on Washington, in the same fall that four girls were killed in the bombing of Birmingham's 16th Street Baptist Church — Baldwin was talking about children he knew, in neighborhoods he had lived in, facing conditions the schools had helped create. He cut to what he called "the entire purpose of education in the first place": "the paradox of education is precisely this — that as one begins to become conscious one begins to examine the society in which he is being educated." That examination is the goal — "to create in a person the ability to look at the world for himself, to make his own decisions... to ask questions of the universe, and then learn to live with those questions." That is democratic education stated plainly. But Baldwin did not stop there. "No society is really anxious to have that kind of person around. What societies really, ideally, want is a citizenry which will simply obey the rules of society. If a society succeeds in this, that society is about to perish. The obligation of anyone who thinks of himself as responsible is to examine society and try to change it and to fight it — at no matter what risk."

Dewey believed schools could be laboratories of democracy. Baldwin believed that too — and he understood what it cost a child who took that education seriously in a society that had never extended its promises to her. The independent mind Dewey wanted the school to produce would, if it was genuinely free, look squarely at what America had done and was doing. That is not a comfortable outcome. It is the democratic one.

In an age of encounter, the stakes of Baldwin's argument are higher, not lower. The child who will share a classroom, a neighborhood, a democracy with people unlike herself needs exactly what Baldwin was demanding — the capacity to examine the world honestly, to ask questions of it, and to act on what she finds. That is not a lesson that can be taught to some children and withheld from others. It is the condition of democratic life when encounter is not occasional but inescapable.

* * *

My elementary school education was a failure in preparing students — myself and my peers — for living in a world of encounter. While the details were different and the composition of the classroom was not the same, Baldwin's prescient critique identified the civic purpose that went unfulfilled. I grew up inside that failure, attending a public school that gathered children across ethnic, cultural, religious, and racial differences and left us entirely alone with it at a time when that was not only irresponsible, it was actually dangerous.

I went to a Jewish Sunday school as a kid. And I hated it. In my memory, I skipped a lot. I never said this to my parents, but it made me feel different, marked, separate from a norm I desperately wanted to belong to. The norm, of course, was one that had no intention of fully accepting me.

My neighborhood was overwhelmingly Irish Catholic. My school was overwhelmingly Irish Catholic. The cultural grammar was Catholic in ways so pervasive they were invisible to those inside it and inescapable to those outside. I understood, without anyone having to explain it, that I was not quite the same as everyone else.

I wanted so badly to belong that I really wanted to change my name. Adam to Sean. I wanted to shed the mark of my difference and slip into the stream of the accepted. My family were the Jews in a big house in a neighborhood that was far less affluent than the rest of the town. Kids called the neighborhood "The Point," which was short for "Whiskey Point" - an anti-Irish slur that my Irish-American classmates claimed for their own.

I was called a kike. I was called a Christ killer. I was teased and bullied in ways that made clear my place in the social order. The school did nothing — or nothing that mattered. It had no language for what was happening, no curriculum that might have helped my classmates understand who I was or where my people came from, no systematic effort to prepare any of us to live together across our differences.

We were not the only family navigating this. Our neighbors, the O'Briens, also lived in a big house, and their kids were targets too. But they were clever enough — or connected enough — to find their way into a different school across town. We stayed.

My Black friends had it worse. The slurs were uglier, the exclusion more total, the violence more real. If the school failed me, it failed them catastrophically.

And this is what I keep returning to: the public school — the institution that claimed as its purpose the preparation of young people for pluralistic democratic life — did not prepare us to live together. It gathered us in the same building and left us to sort it out ourselves. The sorting was brutal. The lessons we learned were not the ones anyone would have chosen to teach.

* * *

This is not a story about the 1970s. It is a story about now.

Reyna Grande wrote her first story in the fifth grade — in Spanish, the only language she knew. Her teacher put it in the reject pile. "In doing so, she rejected me and who I was."

Angela Valenzuela studied a Houston high school in the late 1990s and found that immigrant-origin students who had recently arrived often had more positive relationships with school than their U.S.-born peers. The longer students were exposed to American schooling, the more their social capital eroded. She called it subtractive schooling. Twenty-five years later, the finding still holds.

The pattern my mother lived through in Memphis. The pattern I lived through in Boston. Different decades, different cities, different groups at the sharp end. Same silence. Same erasure. Same bargain: you can be here, but not as who you are.

* * *

So what I am arguing for is not a return. The common school's version of shared life demanded erasure as the price of admission. We cannot go back to that — and we should not want to.

What I am arguing for is a reimagining of the role of education in pluralistic democracies.

There is a difference between education that prepares people to navigate shared space and education built around erasure as a means of creating community. The first says: the commons is a meeting place, and what happens there should transform everyone who enters. The second says: the commons belongs to us, and you may enter if you become like us.

What I am arguing for is the distinction itself, taken seriously at last. Education can and must prepare young people to move through the commons. But the commons is not the property of any single group. It is not a finished inheritance to be accepted. It is a space that must be continually built by everyone who enters it. And entering it does not mean absorbing into it.

WHAT HAPPENS WHEN WE MEET

"Without real interaction, stereotypes fill the void."

In 2006, Robert Putnam delayed publishing some of the most unsettling research of his career. Putnam, the Harvard political scientist who had chronicled America's declining social capital in Bowling Alone, had devoted years to studying diverse communities across the country. What he found disturbed him. In the short term, people living in more diverse neighborhoods trusted their neighbors less — not just neighbors who were different from them, but all their neighbors, including those who looked like them. They withdrew from civic life. They "hunkered down," he called it: "turtling in."

The research has been cited endlessly by people arguing that diversity itself is the problem, that human beings are simply not built to live among those who are different. Yet Putnam's own interpretation was far more subtle. The hunkering down, he argued, was a short-term response. Over the long term, diverse communities developed new forms of social solidarity and new identities capacious enough to include what had once seemed foreign. The discomfort was real, but it was not destiny.

The question Putnam did not answer was what happened in between. What determined whether a community moved through the discomfort toward something better, or got stuck in withdrawal and resentment? What made the difference between short-term anxiety becoming long-term integration, versus short-term anxiety calcifying into permanent division?

This is the question education must answer.

* * *

The research since Putnam has filled in the picture, and it is more complicated than either optimists or pessimists want to believe.

Ryan Enos, also at Harvard, designed an experiment on the Boston commuter rail. He arranged for Spanish-speaking passengers to board trains in predominantly white communities and ride during rush hour, day after day. Then he surveyed the regular commuters about their attitudes toward immigration.

The results seemed to confirm the view that human beings are unable to accept differences. Exposure to Spanish-speaking passengers made commuters more likely to support restrictive immigration policies. Mere presence — not interaction, not conflict, just presence — shifted attitudes in a more hostile direction.

But Enos kept measuring over the next few weeks, and the effect faded. Attitudes returned to baseline. The initial spike of anxiety did not persist.

What does this mean? The encounter was empty. Without any structure — without conversation, cooperation, shared purpose — presence alone accomplished nothing. It produced a reaction, then nothing. But it also did not permanently poison the well.

The pattern holds at every scale. Jens Rydgren and Patrick Ruth mapped all 5,668 voting districts in Sweden and found that hostility toward immigrants flared most intensely not where immigrants actually lived, but in the homogeneous communities nearby — close enough to perceive change, not close enough to complicate it. Jocelyn Evans and Gilles Ivaldi found the same pattern in France. Ryan Enos had found the same thing on a Boston commuter rail platform. The geography of fear is the geography of the imagined other.

The researchers called this the difference between the "experienced other" and the "imagined other." When difference remains abstract — visible from a distance, encountered only through news reports and political rhetoric — it can be filled with whatever fears people carry. When difference becomes concrete — the family next door, the coworker, the parent at school pickup — the abstraction breaks down.

These findings about proximity and encounter were tested dramatically during the 2015–16 refugee crisis in Germany. Across the country, anxiety about refugees spiked. The national mood turned fearful. But Marco Giesselmann, David Brady, and Tabea Naujoks, studying the pattern district by district, found something striking: in the specific places where refugees actually settled, concern about immigration decreased and support for far-right parties fell. The national anxiety was about an imagined threat. Where the encounter was real, the fear diminished.

* * *

Jennifer Richeson's research adds another dimension. She and her colleagues told white Americans that demographic projections showed they would become a minority of the U.S. population by 2042. This information alone — just the demographic fact — shifted attitudes to the right. It increased opposition to diversity policies and, among some participants, warmed attitudes toward the Republican Party.

But framing mattered enormously. When the same demographic information was presented as "growing diversity" rather than "white decline," the anxiety response diminished dramatically. The facts were identical. The story around the facts changed everything.

This is not a finding about fragility or sensitivity. It is a finding about meaning-making. Human beings do not respond to demographic change as raw data. They respond to demographic change as interpreted through narratives — narratives about what the change means, who they are in relation to it, whether it represents threat or opportunity, loss or possibility.

Those narratives are not fixed. They are constructed by politicians, the media, families, and communities. And by schools.

There is a deeper question underneath Richeson's finding that the book needs to answer: why does the encounter with difference produce anxiety in the first place? Where does the fear come from?

Franz Boas, the founder of modern American anthropology, spent his career exploring those questions. What seems like a natural response to people from different backgrounds — the wariness, the withdrawal, the hostility — is not natural; it is learned. Boas called these responses "patterned practices" — emotional habits socialized into our mental makeup through cultural transmission — so deeply embedded that they feel like our own authentic reactions rather than what they actually are: patterns shaped by history, reinforced by the institutions and narratives that surround us. We are taught who to fear and who to trust, who belongs and who doesn't, long before we are old enough to examine those lessons. And because enculturation is implicit, absorbed through a thousand daily messages instead of direct instruction, most of us never examine it at all. My mother used to sing the song, "You've got to be carefully taught to hate" from South Pacific. It's true, just not in the way that she thought.

This matters for the argument this book is making, because it changes what we are asking of education. The anxiety that attends encounter with difference is not a flaw to be corrected. It is more like an immune response — a system doing what systems do when they detect the unfamiliar. The question is not whether the response will fire, but whether it will calibrate correctly: whether it will learn to distinguish the imagined threat from the real one, the unfamiliar from the enemy. An immune system that cannot distinguish self from other becomes autoimmune, attacking what it should protect. One that cannot respond at all leaves the organism defenseless. What we want is neither — we want a system trained to read the signal accurately. That is what education can do. The fear is not destiny. It is a signal that something unfamiliar has entered the picture — and what determines the response is not the signal itself, but the conditions that precede the encounter, shape it, and follow from it.

Schools are precisely positioned to do this work — and have largely failed to do it. The conditions that surround the encounter don't arrange themselves. Someone has to build them. Education — in both its spoken and implicit forms — is that work.

* * *

Years ago, while I was working on a book for Facing History about the treatment of Muslim youth in French schools, I finally read Gordon Allport's The Nature of Prejudice, published in 1954, the same year as Brown v. Board of Education. I wish I had read it sooner.

In the early years of the civil rights movement, Allport was asking: after the Holocaust, after Hiroshima and Nagasaki, after we have seen what human beings are capable of doing to one another, is a different response possible?

His answer was yes. But it was a conditional yes.

Allport's "contact hypothesis" posited that contact between groups, under certain conditions, reduces prejudice. Without the right conditions, contact makes things worse. With them, it transforms how people see one another.

He identified four conditions: equal status between the groups in the situation, common goals that require joint effort, intergroup cooperation rather than competition, and institutional support — the sanction of authorities, laws, or customs that signal the contact is appropriate and expected.

In 2006, Thomas Pettigrew and Linda Tropp demonstrated that he was right. Their meta-analysis of 515 studies involving over 250,000 participants was unambiguous: contact under Allport's conditions reduces prejudice. The effect is consistent and robust. The conditions are the mechanism.

* * *

When you read the research together — Putnam, Enos, Richeson, the Swedish and German studies, Allport — a pattern emerges. It offers no comfort to those who believe diversity will work itself out, and no ammunition to those who argue it is the problem.

Diversity is not the variable that determines whether an encounter goes well or badly. Proximity is not either. The variable is the quality of the interaction — whether the encounter occurs under conditions that foster understanding or those that foster threat.

I have come to think of it as a formula. Xenophobia increases as the rate of demographic change increases and as physical proximity between different groups increases. But xenophobia decreases as the quality of social interaction improves. $X = (R \times 1/D) \div Q$. We cannot control R — the rate of change is driven by forces larger than any policy. We cannot control D — proximity is the reality of modern life. What we can control is Q — the quality of social interaction. And Q is what too few educational leaders are focused on.

* * *

But before we turn to what goes wrong when Q is absent, I need to say something about what the encounter with difference actually is — not in the research literature, but in life.

The Sufi tradition has a word — gharib — that means both "strange" and "wonderful." Fatima Mernissi, the Moroccan feminist scholar, built a whole book around this idea. Her grandmother taught her about lawami' — flashes of illumination that come only at the frontier, only in the encounter with what is unfamiliar. The frontier is not a boundary to be defended. It is the site where knowledge is produced.

I know this from pickup basketball games in the gym, where I was often the only white kid on the court. From sitting as a teenager in La Bonbonnière in the West Village, listening to Percy Johnston — poet, professor, playwright — who opened a door in my mind with lectures over French toast and coffee. From teaching students in Santa Monica who had been involved in gangs, who taught me more about resilience and moral complexity than any graduate seminar. From my Ecuadorian mother-in-law, whose customs were uncomfortable for me at first and whom I came to love, and whose way of organizing family life revealed the narrowness of what I had assumed was universal.

Both things are true. Encounter is where the flashes come from. And encounter, unsupported, is where the fear comes from. The variable that determines which one you get is Q.

* * *

When the planes hit the towers on September 11, 2001, I was working at Facing History and Ourselves. In the aftermath, it became clear that educators had very little practice facilitating conversations across differences — and almost none when it came to religion, terrorism, and the relationship between the two. At a time when a specific, violent distortion of Islamic faith had been used to justify mass murder, most educators did not have the tools to help students understand Islam on its own terms, to distinguish between a religion and those who weaponize it, or to reckon honestly with the hatred and suspicion that fell — in schools, in communities, across the country — on Muslim students, Arab students, South Asian students, Sikh students, on anyone who looked like someone's idea of the enemy. The same pattern that had always filled the absence of understanding now filled it at scale: fear, stereotyping, and the silence of institutions that didn't know what to say and so said nothing. Which taught its own lesson.

The pattern has repeated. The conflict in Israel and Palestine is doing to this generation what Vietnam did fifty years ago — splitting communities, ending friendships, making students feel suspect based on their background or their beliefs. Jewish students are afraid to identify themselves. Palestinian students' identities and experiences erased — their history unmentionable, their grief illegitimate. And in K–12 classrooms across the country, teachers are asking the same questions: Do I say anything? What if it gets out of control? What if I say the wrong thing?

Most choose silence. The silence teaches: some things are too dangerous for this room.

For immigrant-origin students, the stakes are more concrete still. They carry the world with them — not as abstraction but as lived reality. Languages, family histories, and knowledge of places that exist beyond the school's walls. Too often, schools treat this as a problem. The child who speaks Spanish at home is marked as "English Language Learner" — defined by what she lacks rather than what she has.

Here, then, is the full picture of what happens when we meet. Locally: proximity alone does not produce understanding. It can produce withdrawal, anxiety, or hostility — especially when the encounter lacks structure, when difference remains abstract, when narratives of threat dominate. But proximity under the right conditions can reduce prejudice, build perspective-taking capacity, and forge new forms of solidarity.

The conditions are known. Allport identified them seventy years ago. Pettigrew and Tropp confirmed them across 515 studies. Richeson showed us that narrative shapes whether the same facts produce curiosity or fear. The variable we control is Q — the quality of interaction. We know what makes Q high. We know what makes it low. We know what's at stake.

HOW WE FAILED TO BUILD IT

"Deny the conditions. Ensure failure. Cite the failure as evidence."

The previous chapter ended with a question that should trouble us. If we know the conditions under which contact across difference produces understanding — if we can document them, measure them, replicate them — why has the institution best positioned to create those conditions largely stopped trying?

The answer is not one story. It is two — running in parallel, reinforcing each other, producing the crisis we are living through.

The first story is about the conditions being deliberately denied. The second is about the institution being led away from its purpose.

I. The Conditions Denied

In 1954 — the same year Allport published — the Supreme Court decided Brown v. Board of Education. The legal and psychological questions converged. If schools were desegregated, what would determine whether contact produced understanding or conflict?

Allport's conditions offered an answer, and a warning. Desegregation by itself would accomplish nothing. Or, the backlash might even make things worse. But desegregation designed with Allport's conditions in mind — equal status, common goals, cooperation, institutional support — had a real shot at success.

What followed the Court's decision was resistance — but I want to be precise about what that means. Governors chose to defy federal courts. State legislators chose to pass laws designed to evade or delay. School board members chose to drag their feet. And across the South, white parents faced a choice: send their children to school alongside Black children, or find some other way. Many of them found other ways.

In 1957, when nine Black students attempted to enroll at Central High School in Little Rock, the governor chose to call out the National Guard to block them. President Eisenhower had to send federal troops to escort those nine teenagers past a mob threatening to lynch them and into the school.

Think about what the Little Rock Nine actually walked into, in Allport's terms. Equal status? Not only were they stereotyped as inferior, but they were also positioned as intruders from the moment they arrived. Common goals? The Black students wanted what every student should want: an education. But the white students and their families were not focused on education. They were focused on exclusion. Cooperation? The opposite. Harassment, isolation, violence. Minnijean Brown was expelled for retaliating after months of abuse — for finally fighting back against tormentors who faced no consequences. Institutional support? The governor called out the National Guard to block them.

Every condition Allport identified as necessary for productive contact was systematically denied. I should be clear, this was not an accident. It was a strategy.

The segregationists understood something: if you let the conditions for successful integration be constructed, integration might succeed. If Black and white children actually worked together toward common goals, as equals, with institutional support, they might come to see each other as legitimate participants in shared life. They might form friendships. They might discover that the categories that divided them were less important than the humanity they shared. In the middle of the crisis, a reporter interviewed an anonymous 16-year-old white female student at Central High who explained, "If parents would just go home and let us alone, we'll be all right...We just want them to leave us be. We can do it."

This was precisely what segregationists feared most. Not that integration would fail, but that it might work. Their fear was explicit and intimate: that Black and white children growing up together would come to know each other as equals, form friendships, fall in love. The violence at Little Rock was designed to ensure that the transition would fail — that contact would be traumatic, that the encounter would produce withdrawal and hostility, that the whole experiment could be declared a disaster. And when even that failed, they did the only thing left: they closed the schools entirely. In 1958, Governor Faubus shuttered all four Little Rock high schools rather than allow integration to take root.

The violence at Little Rock was designed to ensure that the transition would fail — that contact would be traumatic, that the encounter would produce withdrawal and hostility, that the whole experiment could be declared a disaster. And when the contact produced exactly the trauma it was designed to produce, segregationists could point to the failure as proof that integration itself was the problem. Deny the conditions. Ensure failure. Cite the failure as evidence. The strategy was never fully successful. Imperfect, contested, and painfully slow, school integration did open doors — new relationships formed, new possibilities emerged that the segregationists had feared most. We are living through the backlash now.

* * *

My mother was sixteen that year, attending a private school in Memphis. She watched the news from Little Rock like everyone else. But then something happened closer to home.

The white families fleeing Little Rock's public schools needed somewhere to send their children. Some of them sent them to my mother's school. The enrollment swelled with white kids fleeing desegregation.

My grandmother saw what was happening. These were families who had chosen to pull their children out of public school rather than let them sit in classrooms with Black students. And now they were filling up the school where her own daughters sat.

She made a choice. Her daughters would not remain in a school, becoming a refuge for those who fled the encounter with difference. She pulled my mother and her sister out and enrolled them in public school.

It was a small act. It changed nothing about the larger pattern. But it taught my mother something about what her family stood for, even when standing was costly.

* * *

What followed the Court's decision reveals a lot about the possibilities and barriers to and of belonging. In some places, desegregation was met with the kind of resistance that dominates our collective memory. But in other places, there were signs of what's possible when we commit to breaking down bigotry.

Charlotte, North Carolina, became a national model. After the Supreme Court's 1971 Swann decision upheld busing as a remedy for segregation, Charlotte-Mecklenburg Schools implemented one of the most comprehensive desegregation plans in the country. The results, documented over decades, were striking. Black students showed dramatic gains in academic achievement. White students were not harmed. The system worked for more than twenty years before political forces dismantled it.

Economist Rucker Johnson, in his landmark study Children of the Dream, tracked students from the first attempts at integration through to today's re-segregation. His findings were clear: African Americans who attended desegregated, well-funded schools experienced dramatic improvements in educational attainment, earnings, and health — and these improvements did not come at the expense of white students. The benefits were inter-generational.

Johnson's research revealed something else: the high point of school integration in America was 1988. Since then, we have been moving backward. By some measures, American schools are more segregated today than they were in the 1970s. This is not because desegregation failed. It is because we stopped trying.

In 1974, the Supreme Court decided Milliken v. Bradley. A federal judge in Detroit concluded that desegregation within the city limits was mathematically impossible: there simply were not enough white students left. The only solution was a metropolitan plan that included suburban districts. Ignoring the demographic reality, the Supreme Court argued that such a solution was unconstitutional. The city had to solve its own problems.

Justice Thurgood Marshall wrote a dissent that reads now like prophecy: "Unless our children begin to learn together, there is little hope that our people will ever learn to live together and understand each other."

Where desegregation was genuinely implemented — where the conditions were constructed, where leadership supported the effort, where resources followed the commitment — the research shows it worked. What failed was not the idea. What failed was the commitment.

II. The Institution Led Astray

The failure to build the conditions for a productive encounter with difference was not only about desegregation. It was also about the narrowing of what schools understood themselves to be for.

The 1960s and early 1970s were a period of extraordinary ferment in American education. The civil rights movement had forced a national reckoning about racism, justice, equity, and democracy. The Vietnam War raised urgent questions about citizenship and conscience. A generation of educators began experimenting with approaches that took seriously the idea that education was about more than transmitting information. Values clarification. Moral development. Peace education. Multicultural education.

Lawrence Kohlberg, at Harvard, was developing his theory of moral development — the idea that ethical reasoning could be cultivated through education. Carol Gilligan challenged and complicated his framework. The conversation was rich, contested, and alive. People believed it mattered.

I know this because these were not abstract figures to me. My mother was a student of Kohlberg's and a friend of Gilligan's. Their debates — about justice, gender, and care, about how moral reasoning develops, about what schools owed young people — were conversations in my house in my living room. While I remember them, mainly I remember wanting them to pay attention to me. Looking back, I should have paid more attention to them.

This was the intellectual environment in which my mother began her work. She was a teacher in Brookline, Massachusetts, frustrated by a curriculum that both explicitly promoted sexist stereotypes while ignoring the Holocaust and the Nazi dismantling of democracy. She started small, developing materials with colleagues, testing them with students. From those classroom experiments, Facing History and Ourselves grew.

Then the backlash came.

It came from multiple directions. Conservatives who saw values education as liberal indoctrination. Parents who felt moral education belonged to the family and the church. Educators worn down by the conflicts of the era, eager for something simpler, something measurable. It came from white supremacists who sent us terrifying postcards.

My mother's organization became a target. As Melinda Fine documented in Habits of Mind, the attack played out through the U.S. Department of Education itself. In 1980, a review panel cited Facing History as "exemplary." Then, in 1986, when the organization applied for a modest dissemination grant, a panelist named Christina Jeffrey wrote that the program lacked "balance and objectivity" because "the Nazi point of view, however unpopular, is still a point of view and is not presented, nor is that of the Ku Klux Klan."

Let that sit for a moment. A program cited as "exemplary" by the same department six years earlier was being rejected because it did not tell the story from the point of view of racists and antisemites.

It got worse. Phyllis Schlafly lobbied to reject the program. Other reviewers called the curriculum "leftist," "anti-war, anti-hunting," and "profoundly offensive to fundamentalists and evangelicals." In the end, Shirley Curry — a former president of Schlafly's Eagle Forum — eliminated the entire funding category: "History, Geography, and Civics." Think about that for a second, she defunded the category itself rather than allow a program exploring the Holocaust and its moral and ethical implications on human behavior to receive a grant.

The parallels to the present are difficult to ignore. The weaponization of the Department of Education against programs that teach young people to think critically about history, democracy, and difference is not new. It's thoroughly documented in my mother's papers, which are now at the University of Illinois.

The backlash was in response to two transformations that were making schools' civic purpose more urgent, not less. The first was demographic. In 1965, Congress passed the Immigration and Naturalization Act, abolishing the national-origins quota system. Immigration surged. Communities began changing rapidly. Schools were being asked to do exactly what Allport described: create the conditions under which people from different backgrounds could meet as equals and build shared understanding. But they were being asked to do this precisely when the civic tools for doing so were being dismantled.

The second transformation was economic. The 1983 report A Nation at Risk reframed education's purpose in terms that would dominate policy for four decades. Schools existed to produce workers. Workers needed skills. Skills could be measured. The civic purpose of education was not rejected so much as rendered invisible.

Standards beget standardized tests. Tests begat accountability systems. Accountability systems begat high stakes. And high stakes changed everything. What gets measured gets done. What doesn't get measured gets squeezed out. Historical thinking, ethical reasoning, civic capacity, the ability to navigate difference — disappeared from the agenda.

No Child Left Behind made this logic federal policy. Race to the Top doubled down. The education reform movement spoke the language of equity while systematically stripping schools of the mandate to pursue the deeper purposes that equity actually requires.

The result of all this — the conditions denied, the backlash, the narrowing, the business logic — is that the civic purpose of education has been progressively hollowed out.

American classrooms are more diverse than at any point in the nation's history. One in four students has a direct connection to immigration. Students in a single classroom may represent a dozen countries, a dozen languages, a dozen different relationships to the very concept of America.

Civic education survives, but it is often thin, focusing on facts about how a bill becomes a law and the three branches of government. It is too frequently civic education as information transfer, not civic education as capacity building. It prepares students to pass a test about democracy. It does not prepare them to practice it.

There are coalitions and organizations working to change this — I am a member of some of them, and I believe in the effort. But even within these networks, the gap between stated commitments to inclusion and actual practice around immigrant-origin students frustrates me. Citizenship as a legal category and civic capacity as an educational goal are not the same thing, and too few civic education initiatives have reckoned honestly with that distinction.

I am not arguing that academic achievement doesn't matter. What I am arguing is that test scores became a substitute for measuring the holistic outcomes of schools on students. I believe the substitution has been catastrophic; not everyone would agree. In my opinion, it has left us with schools that can produce students who read at grade level but cannot navigate a conversation with someone who sees the world differently. It has left us profoundly unprepared for this moment.

FIELD NOTE I

"Every time a student came alive around a question that mattered, I could see what his education should have been all along–and hadn't been."

Educators are hungry. Not for food and coffee, though they'll take both. I've spoken to tens of thousands of educators over the last 30 years, and it is clear to me that most see the profession as a calling, not simply a job. Although it can sound pretentious to name it, they see their roles as caretakers of community. The best teachers thrive on a balance of democratic passion and deep care for the children in their care.

I have seen it hundreds of times over three decades — in hotel ballrooms and school libraries, in summer institutes and after-school workshops. Teachers arrive carrying something they cannot name, or can name only in private, to a trusted colleague, and after the door is closed. They entered this profession because they believed education could be transformative. They believed they could help young people make sense of the world. And the profession has spent years telling them that it is not their job.

When someone finally says, "Your instinct was right, the questions you want to ask are the questions that matter," something breaks open. I have watched it happen so many times that I can feel it coming. The relief. The recognition. The anger, sometimes, at how long they were told to stand aside for tests, for technology, for whatever reform arrived next. These feelings cross every demographic line I can identify. Rural and urban. Veteran and novice. Conservative and progressive. It is not about politics. It is about purpose.

I first saw it at Facing History and Ourselves. My mother built the organization on the premise that educators deserved to be treated as the professionals that they are, and that studying the worst of human behavior might illuminate the best of human possibility. That history, taught well, is not about the past but about moral reasoning in the present. That the question is not only "what happened?" but "what would I have done?" — and that young people, given the tools and the trust, will grapple with that question with a seriousness that puts most adults to shame.

Before I joined the organization, I was teaching in a self-contained classroom at Santa Monica High School. There were three of us for 11 students — all boys who had been failed by the system, waiting for their eighteenth birthday. Almost all of them were in gangs and all of them came from communities torn apart by gang violence. For those who associate Santa Monica with its more familiar reputation, this may be hard to believe. That's probably not an accident. Our students weren't allowed to take classes, even gym, in the rest of the building. Even as teachers, we were isolated from the rest of our colleagues.

There was a drive-by at the end of school one day. I was unlocking my bike and had to hit the sidewalk. It was terrifying. The students were electric the next day — the fear and trauma masked, or at least submerged. But nobody created any space to talk about it, or if they did, I didn't know about it, and our students were certainly not invited. As I remember it, my two colleagues and I were left to figure out what to do on our own.

From across the country, my mother would send me things to try with the students — short stories, videos, readings she thought I might use to open up conversation. Boys who had shut down began reflecting on power and violence, racism and conformity. They lit up when we explored big ideas — not because the ideas were abstract but because they were real. They thought I was moralizing when I explained that, where and when I grew up, there were no gangs. We talked about belonging, identity, and what it means to be safe. As someone who grew up in a city with such racial division, I didn't understand why the children of Mexican immigrants were caught up in a system of "us" and "them" that divided the community by street, block, and neighborhood. My ignorance, I think, gave them permission to question the systems around them. And I learned from them too, not just about gangs and violence, but about culture and history. They loved teaching me Spanish expressions and laughed when I would selectively use them.

Despite the joy that came from building relationships with these challenging, often incredibly kind, but ultimately vulnerable young men, I had no training and no real strategies for processing the trauma of their lives. I'd sleep for hours in the afternoon before waking up to make dinner.

Teaching was like jazz, except I didn't really know how to play the instrument. It was all instincts. The conversations were important, serious, and reflective. But they were not enough to make up for what had come before — years of accumulated failure, of an education system that had written these boys off long before they ended up in my room. Every time a student came alive around a question that mattered, I could see what his education should have been all along — and hadn't been.

I left Santa Monica carrying that question with me. Eleven years later, working at Facing History and Ourselves, a different kind of crisis would show me how much larger it was than any single classroom. On September 12, my mother pulled me aside and asked me to write a resource for educators — something that could help them explore the roots of the violence that had just shaken our world.

The events of that day and those that followed brought the world into classrooms that were not ready for it. September 11 forced an encounter with a world most of us knew little about. We didn't know the history, the culture, the geography, the context. What we did know was often incomplete — shaped by media, by stereotypes, by decades of absence from the curriculum. The Middle East had been taught as ancient history. Islam, like almost every religion in the American curriculum, had been taught as a set of practices and beliefs rather than as a living force — one that shapes how people think, how they raise their children, how they organize their communities, how they understand justice and belonging and the boundaries of public life. That gap in understanding was enormous, particularly for making sense of communities, in the United States and around the world, where religion is not a private matter but the very fabric of daily life. Schools had long avoided the subject — too contested, too personal, too likely to offend someone. That silence left students without the tools to understand what they were watching, and it left teachers without the tools to help them.

From what I could tell, most of my colleagues had never knowingly met a Muslim. In the absence of knowledge and context, everything was to be explained by religion — but most of us had never been taught to think about religion as a discipline, only as a matter of ritual or private faith. How, then, were we supposed to understand, let alone teach, the use of religion to justify mass murder? And what about the Muslim and Arab students sitting in those classrooms, now subjected to the fear and misunderstanding of their peers — and often their teachers?

My colleague Sara K. Ahmed is one of those special educators who makes every student feel seen — someone who has spent her career helping young people find themselves in texts, in history, in each other. She lived September 11 from both sides, as a teacher and as a Muslim American, carrying the weight of both at once. She described it this way: "Soon after the news broke on 9/11 the American public retaliated against their fellow citizens... people who were born here like me, maybe like you. People who pledge allegiance to the flag, who vote, who study, who pay taxes — who have a name similar to mine... or the visibility of a beard similar to my father's, a headscarf like my aunt's. Even towards men who wear turbans — they are Sikhs, a completely different religion." Another colleague described something harder still — her own son had pulled off her headscarf, so internalized was the shame directed at his mother that he became the instrument of it.

Some teachers struggled to separate their own religious perspectives from their professional role — and some didn't think they needed to. That too was a failure of preparation, not only of individual judgment. Schools had given teachers no framework for thinking about religion as a subject, so when the moment arrived, they had only their own convictions to draw on.

In this moment, my mother and I wanted young people to do something harder than reach for easy answers. We wanted them to recognize what was particular about this moment, and to find within it the patterns that recur across time and place — how religion gets used and misused, how fear produces scapegoats, how belonging gets drawn and redrawn. But the question that our colleagues kept pushing was larger: how do you provide professional learning at the scale the moment demanded?

* * *

What I saw in that crisis — and in every crisis since — was the gap between what schools needed and what any outside organization's resources and professional learning modules can authentically provide.

What I came to see over time was that the teachers who sustained this work for years were the ones whose administrators understood what they were doing and protected the space for it. The ones who burned out were the ones doing it alone, against the grain, without institutional support. This is Allport's fourth condition, made personal: institutional support is not an abstraction. It is the principal who says "keep going" when a parent complains, or the test scores don't always match expectations.

I carry enormous pride in my work at Facing History. But I also carry something else. The recognition that the content our team created was bold and important. However, being bold is not the same as being culturally responsive to changing classrooms and communities. As we scaled — as we sought to prove our impact — the institutional pressure shifted toward fidelity to an increasingly sequenced and standardized curriculum rather than responsiveness to students. That pressure came from both inside and outside of the organization. For my team, it meant developing curriculum designed to be delivered with the same beats, resources, and assessments in every classroom. I believed then, as I believe now, that a teacher who knew her community and her students, and found a resource, primary source, teaching strategy, or guiding question better suited to her classroom should use it. I see that as essential to being culturally responsive. But fidelity and responsiveness pull in different directions, and scale almost always wins.

Meanwhile, something had quietly shifted. Content was no longer scarce — the web had seen to that — but abundance created its own problem. Every teacher now had access to everything, which meant every teacher had to decide what mattered. What was scarce, it turned out, was not material but the capacity to look at your changing community and choose the questions, the conversations, the primary sources that your students actually needed. That is a different kind of professional knowledge than curriculum delivery. And it was rarely taught. A national organization can write a unit. It cannot know what your students carried into the room that morning.

I did not have the answer when I left Facing History. What I had was a clearer sense of what the answer could not be. It could not come from the outside in. Whatever it was, it had to start closer to the ground. The question I left with: what would it take to build belonging from the inside out?

PART II

The Seeds

THE CAPACITIES WE NEED

"Belonging is not a feeling to cultivate after the real work is done. It is a cognitive precondition–the foundation without which the real work cannot happen."

The encounter with difference is a permanent feature of the human experience. However, as we've explored, it doesn't mean that we have an innate ability to turn encounters into productive engagement. The research is clear about what makes the difference between an encounter that produces understanding and one that produces fear. And schools — the institution best positioned to act on that research — have not been oriented towards this vital work.

So, what would it actually take?

Not a program. Not a curriculum package. Not one more initiative added to an already-crowded plate. What it would take is a tradition of thought that has been answering this question for decades — largely unheeded by the policymakers who narrowed education's purpose and the philanthropists who funded the narrowing.

— — —

John Dewey understood the foundation a century ago. "The intermingling in the school of youth of different races, differing religions, and unlike customs," he wrote in 1916, "creates for all a new and broader environment." Democracy, he argued, is not a form of government. It is a mode of associated living — of conjoint communicated experience. Education is not preparation for democratic life. It is democratic life in its formative stage.

This means something specific for schools. The classroom is not a place where young people learn about democracy and then go practice it somewhere else. The classroom is the place where they practice it — where they learn to navigate shared problems across difference, to find common cause without demanding sameness, to hold disagreement without collapse.

Dewey was not theorizing from a distance. He had spent time at Hull House with Jane Addams, immersed in one of the most diverse neighborhoods in America, part of a movement that recognized what immigration was doing to — and for — the country. He envisioned a democracy expansive enough to embrace newcomers, Jews and Catholics specifically, and believed schools were the institution that could ensure everyone participated on equal footing. He had worked alongside Anzia Yezierska, the Jewish immigrant writer from the Lower East Side whose fiction captured what it felt like to arrive in America hungry for belonging. Yezierska was drawn to his vision, and he to her world. Their relationship was complicated — and her writing suggests she understood, from the inside, something his philosophy struggled to accommodate: that the promise of democratic fellowship looked different depending on where you stood when you received it.

His vision was radical, and it remains influential. But Dewey was a philosopher, not a curriculum designer or a school administrator — and the gap between his ideas and the experience of the people his ideas were ostensibly for has never been fully closed.

Paulo Freire answered from a different place. Writing from Brazil in 1968, Freire argued that education is never neutral. It either functions as an instrument of conformity — integrating the young into the logic of the existing system — or it becomes the practice of freedom, the means by which people engage critically with reality and discover their power to transform it. There is no middle ground.

Dewey gives you the aspiration. Freire gives you the critique. What followed was a generation of scholars and educators who developed a pedagogy that could deliver on both.

* * *

Educators need to sustain students' identities, not erase them. This is not only a matter of justice, though it is that. It is a precondition for the encounter with difference to work at all. A student who has been taught to hide or abandon who they are cannot bring themselves to the encounter — cannot offer what they carry, cannot receive what others bring. And when students do bring themselves fully — when they study together, work together, play together, live alongside one another — what moves between them is not just tolerance but genuine exchange. Identity sustaining is not the opposite of bridge building. It is what makes bridge building real. A generation of researchers, working mostly from the margins of American education, built the evidence for why — and what it looks like in practice.

Claude Steele's research identified what he called "stereotype threat" — the anxiety that arises when a person is in a situation where they might confirm a negative stereotype about their group. A Black student taking a math test, a woman in a physics classroom, a Latino student in a gifted program — the mere awareness that a negative stereotype exists creates a cognitive burden that degrades performance. "No amount of instruction, no matter how good it is, can reduce these deficits if it doesn't also keep identity threat low," Steele wrote. "Without that, threat will always have first claim on students' attention and mental resources."

Rudine Sims Bishop, writing about children's literature in 1990, gave us the metaphor that has shaped two generations of educators: books as windows, mirrors, and sliding glass doors. Students need to see themselves reflected in the curriculum. They also need windows into lives different from their own. And they need sliding glass doors — the invitation to walk through into a genuine encounter with the other.

Gloria Ladson-Billings asked a different question. Where most researchers asked what was wrong with Black students who were failing, she asked what was right with Black students who were succeeding. The answer became culturally relevant pedagogy: academic rigor AND cultural competence, and sociopolitical consciousness. All three. Not a choice among them.

Django Paris pushed further. Being relevant to students' cultures was not the same as actively sustaining those cultures through schooling. Culturally sustaining pedagogy, he argued, "seeks to perpetuate and foster — to sustain — linguistic, literate, and cultural pluralism as part of the democratic project of schooling." The goal of education is not to produce standardized citizens sanded down to acceptable sameness but to cultivate people deeply rooted in their own traditions while genuinely curious about others.

Luis Moll, Norma González, and Cathy Amanti went into the homes of students in Tucson — mostly low-income Mexican and Mexican-American families that schools had written off as deficient. Their premise was simple and radical: "People are competent and have knowledge, and their life experiences have given them that knowledge." They called these "funds of knowledge" — the accumulated wisdom that families possess from their labor, their traditions, their survival.

Gholdy Muhammad went looking for the historical roots and found them in the 19th-century Black literary societies. These communities organized themselves around identity, skills, intellect, and what Muhammad calls criticality — the capacity to read the world, recognize injustice, and act — building the educational infrastructure that institutions denied them, without waiting for anyone's permission. Muhammad titled her book Cultivating Genius — not remediating deficits.

And Zaretta Hammond brought the neuroscience. Culture, she showed, shapes how brains process information — how they build schema, encode memory, make meaning. When a student's cultural knowledge is dismissed as irrelevant, the brain has nothing to hook new learning onto. When that knowledge is honored and activated, learning accelerates.

* * *

Now I need to say something plainly that the research has been showing us from every angle, because the failure to say it plainly has allowed people to treat belonging as a luxury — as something nice to have after the real work of education is done.

Belonging is the precondition for everything else schools are trying to accomplish.

This is not a claim about feelings. It is a claim about how human beings function — cognitively, socially, and civically.

Carol Goodenow began measuring it in the early 1990s, developed the Psychological Sense of School Membership scale, and demonstrated that belonging was significantly associated with academic motivation. Students who felt they belonged tried harder, expected more of themselves, and cared more about what they were learning. Students who did not belong withdrew — not because they lacked ability but because the environment had failed to hold them.

Gregory Walton and Geoffrey Cohen at Stanford took the research further. In a landmark 2011 study published in Science, they designed a brief intervention — just 1 hour — that addressed belonging uncertainty among African American college freshmen. The results were extraordinary. Over the next three years, the intervention halved the racial achievement gap in GPA. It improved students' self-reported health and well-being. It reduced the number of doctor visits. And when Walton and Brady followed up years later, they found the effects had persisted into adulthood.

What Walton's research revealed is the mechanism. When students are uncertain about whether they belong, they interpret ordinary setbacks — a bad grade, a difficult conversation, a moment of social awkwardness — as confirmation that they do not. Each setback deepens the uncertainty. The uncertainty degrades performance. The degraded performance produces more setbacks. The cycle is vicious.

The evidence converges from every direction. Belonging predicts academic outcomes — not just grades but motivation, effort, persistence, and the willingness to take intellectual risks. Belonging predicts social outcomes — the capacity to form relationships, collaborate, navigate conflict, and trust. And belonging predicts civic outcomes — the dispositions this entire book is about.

* * *

This is where the research about contact theory and the liberatory tradition of culturally relevant, responsive, and sustaining practices converge — and where this book's central insight becomes visible.

Let's return to Allport's four conditions translated into classroom reality.

What does equal status actually look like between a kid whose family has been here for four generations and a kid who arrived from Guatemala last year? It doesn't mean pretending the differences don't exist. It means designing the interaction so that both students bring something essential to a shared endeavor. This is Moll and González's insight made structural.

Read Allport alongside Paris. Read Richeson alongside Moll. Read the encounter research and the liberatory tradition together, and something becomes visible that neither field has fully named on its own.

The conditions for productive encounter and for culturally sustaining education are the same.

Equal status is what Moll and González describe when they say that families are experts. Common goals are what Ladson-Billings means by sociopolitical consciousness. Cooperation is what Paris means by sustenance. Institutional support is what all of these thinkers have demanded and what Chapter 4 documented as systematically withdrawn.

The contact theory researchers don't cite the culturally responsive practice scholars. The culturally responsive practice scholars don't use contact theory. They have been working in parallel for decades, across different departments and at different conferences, publishing in different journals. But they are describing the same architecture from different angles. And the architecture is the same.

The convergence is not invisible to everyone. Linda Tropp, who, with Pettigrew, confirmed Allport's hypothesis across 515 studies, has spent the last decade bringing contact theory into schools — documenting how intergroup contact prepares young people to thrive in a multiracial society, and increasingly connecting that research to belonging, inclusion, and equality. Her work has moved the encounter research toward educational practice in ways that make what I am describing here more visible.

But the two traditions — contact theory and culturally sustaining pedagogy — still largely operate in separate worlds, published in different journals, presented at different conferences, read by different audiences. The synthesis remains incomplete.

The field evidence confirms this. Immigrant-origin students lose belonging the longer they're in U.S. schools. This is Angela Valenzuela's finding from 1999, still true a quarter-century later. The system erodes what it should build.

YouthTruth, in partnership with Re-Imagining Migration and the Immigration Initiative at Harvard, surveyed more than 3,000 students and found something that should stop every educator in their tracks. Immigrant-origin students who were discouraged from using their home languages and pressured to assimilate reported the lowest sense of belonging of any group in the study. Immigrant-origin students who were encouraged to bring their whole selves — their languages, their family stories, their cultural knowledge — reported the highest. The difference was not between immigrant and native-born students. It was between two different things that schools chose to do.

And then there is the finding that stops me every time I encounter it. In a five-year longitudinal study of more than 400 newly arrived immigrant students across twenty public schools in Boston, Cambridge, and the San Francisco Bay Area, Carola Suárez-Orozco, Marcelo Suárez-Orozco, and Irina Todorova found that only 6% could name a teacher they would go to with a problem. Just 3% could identify a teacher who was proud of them. Six percent. Three percent. This is the failure of the infrastructure that the entire tradition demands.

Belonging is not a soft skill. It is not an add-on, an enrichment activity, or a program to adopt. It is civic infrastructure — the precondition for participation, not the byproduct.

The capacities are teachable. They require conditions. Schools can construct those conditions.

WHAT THIS LOOKS LIKE

"You cannot scale a relationship. You can scale the conditions that make relationships possible."

Before I describe what this work looks like in schools, I want to start somewhere else — in a tenement on the Lower East Side of Manhattan, in the early years of my career, when I was running programs at the Tenement Museum.

The museum preserves actual tenement apartments as they were lived in by immigrant families in the late nineteenth and early twentieth centuries — cramped, cold-water flats that housed waves of newcomers arriving from Southern and Eastern Europe. Jewish families, Italian families, German families, Polish families. Since I worked there, they have opened additional apartments featuring stories of a Black family on the Lower East Side in the 19th century, as well as Chinese and Puerto Rican immigrants. The same building, different generations, similar struggles: how do you hold onto who you are while becoming someone new?

Visitors came in carrying their own relationships to that history. Many were descendants of the families who had lived in the neighborhood — grandchildren and great-grandchildren of the people in the photographs on the walls. They often arrived with a particular kind of nostalgia, a desire to preserve their ancestors' immigration stories as myth rather than reality. The neighborhood outside had changed. Where were the old Jewish delis, the Italian bakeries, the familiar storefronts? Some visitors came in complaining — the neighborhood felt different, dirtier, less safe. Not what it used to be.

I would have to find a way to say, gently, that communities move on. They evolve. And many of the people living in this neighborhood now — whatever their origins, wherever their families came from — are navigating the same tensions their own relatives navigated ninety years ago. The same push and pull between keeping tradition and fitting in. The same negotiation between acculturation and assimilation. The same question: can I belong here without becoming someone else entirely?

To make that real, I would sometimes show visitors how the neighborhood they were romanticizing had been described when their own families lived there. Jacob Riis, whose photographs of the Lower East Side are among the most famous documents of that era, wrote about it this way, "Today, three-fourths of its people live in the tenements, and the nineteenth-century drift of the population to the cities is sending ever-increasing multitudes to crowd them... Nothing is left but to make the best of a bad bargain."

The "bad bargain" Riis described was the neighborhood that visitors were now mourning. And his language about the people who lived there was worse than his language about the buildings. Of Jewish residents, he wrote, "Thrift is at once its strength and its fatal weakness, its cardinal virtue and its foul disgrace." Of Chinese immigrants, he described them as resembling cats in their "cruel cunning and savage fury." Of Italians, he cited a charity worker who explained that "no one asked for Italian children" — and so none could be sent to the country for fresh air.

The people in those photographs, the ancestors visitors were so proud of, were the people whom those who held power feared, blamed, and caricatured. The "old neighborhood" they missed was, to those who held power in the city at the time, a problem to be solved — its residents considered dangerous, dirty, unassimilable. Not so different from the language used about newcomers today.

Watching visitors sit with that — recognizing their family's story in language that could have been written about any newcomer in any era — was its own kind of education. The contempt didn't belong to the past. The story wasn't over. And the people outside on the street, navigating a city that wasn't entirely sure it wanted them either, were living the same chapter.

Opening those conversations — watching visitors make the connection between the faces in the photographs and the faces outside on the street — produced something I came to recognize as the moment the museum was actually for. Not the preserved artifacts, as extraordinary as they were. The encounter between past and present. The recognition that the story wasn't over.

One morning, I was leading a tour for a school group. A girl, maybe ten or eleven years old, was studying the photographs of the tenement apartments. The cold-water flats. The shared outhouses. The entire family is in two rooms. In addition, there were boarders who used the apartment during the day when the family was at work.

"These folks were really poor, weren't they?" she said.

Yes, I told her. Many of them came to the United States with very little money, doing the best they could to take care of their families and survive.

She looked closer. "They didn't really have anything, did they. Cold water, no windows." She paused. "Are you sure they were Jews?"

I said yes. She said she had no idea that Jews were ever so poor. So we talked about Jewish American history, the Lower East Side economy, and what it meant to arrive with nothing and build something. She was genuinely intrigued. And then she asked a question I have thought about many times since.

"Did the families who lived in the tenement ever see how much money and how much stuff the rich people had?"

It was a great question. We talked through it — about transportation, about newspapers, about what you could and couldn't see from where you stood. And then she concluded something I was not expecting.

"These folks had far less stuff than I have. No TV, no computers, no hot water. No privacy. But I think I am more poor."

I asked why she said that.

"I see, all day long, how much stuff everyone else has. In advertisements, on TV, everywhere. It's like we are constantly told that we are poor because we don't have what they have."

She was ten years old. She had just derived, from a primary-source encounter with history, an insight into relative deprivation and media saturation that most adults take years to articulate. The tenement apartment had become a mirror. And the mirror had shown her something not only about the past but about her own life — and about the structures shaping it.

That is what this education in an age of encounter looks like when it is working.

* * *

The Tenement Museum taught me something about encounter across time — how the past can crack open the present if you create the right conditions. But the most important encounters happen in real time, in the room, with the people actually there.

Years before I cofounded Re-Imagining Migration, I was invited to lead a session at a secondary school in the United Kingdom — not long after the 7/7 bombings in London. The staff was welcoming. The class was fairly diverse. Before I got started, a few teachers pulled me aside. They pointed out a teenage boy sitting near the front. They noted his Islamic prayer beads. One of them told me he was going to become a terrorist.

I wish I could say with certainty that I challenged them in that moment. The rush to get started, the pressure of the room — I'm not sure I handled it as well as I should have. What I do know is that when the class got going, the young man was among its most engaged participants — reflecting seriously on themes of identity, stereotyping, and belonging that I introduced through a clip from the short film Luton, Actually, by the author and journalist Sarfraz Manzoor. A film about a British Muslim navigating exactly the kind of world those teachers had just demonstrated to me.

After class, the young man came straight up and thanked me. He explained that the film was the first time he could remember a teacher ever showing a brown person — in this case, a Muslim — in a classroom lesson.

I told him I understood, though I knew my version was different. That in my own schooling, I had never encountered a Jewish person in any text or lesson until we read the Diary of Anne Frank — which, as powerful as that book is, was a strange first exposure. To meet your own people, for the first time in a classroom, as victims. As history. As the already-dead.

That was his point exactly. Representation matters.

You don't know where those moments go. But there we were — a young British Muslim and a Jewish American educator, standing at the intersection of curriculum and relationship, each carrying a version of the same absence. What a school chooses to teach and who it chooses to make visible are not separate questions. They are the same question. And the answer shapes not only what students learn but whether they believe the room was ever meant for them.

The teachers who pulled me aside were not villains. They were people who had absorbed a narrative — about who was dangerous, who was suspect, who didn't quite belong — and had never been given the tools to examine it. That is a failure of their education, not only their character. As educators, we cannot rely on the stereotypes our culture hands us. If we are going to teach perspective-taking, we have to be capable of it ourselves — which means doing the harder work of examining our own assumptions about our students, their lives, and the communities in which we teach.

The young man taught me that in five minutes after class. I wonder if anyone ever taught it to his teachers.

* * *

I have seen the same dynamic in rooms full of educators.

The first time I led what would become the Moving Stories exercise, I was running a professional development session for teachers in the Boston Public Schools Office of English Learners. We were waiting for a storytelling app to be finalized, so I had to improvise. The protocol was simple — almost embarrassingly so. Carola Suárez-Orozco had developed a set of interview questions about migration and belonging, which I adapted and pared down. I asked the educators to pair up and interview each other. Ten minutes each. The instructions were minimal: ask a question, let the other person decide how much or how little to share, and then — this was the only real rule — listen. Don't respond, don't redirect, don't fill the silence. Just listen until they finish.

I had no idea how it would go. This was the first time.

Almost immediately, the room turned into a roar. I made my way around and saw teachers from everywhere — immigrants and non-immigrants, Black, white, Asian, Latino, from elementary schools and middle schools and high schools — and heard it too: Haitian Creole lilting under the English, Dominican Spanish, the flat vowels of the legendary Boston accent, languages and cadences from across the city and across the world, all of them animated, all leaning in, all visibly moved.

It was the last activity of the day. As I was cleaning up, two teachers came over to thank me. One was a Black woman whose family was from St. Kitts. The other was a white Irish-American woman whose family had been in Boston for generations. I know this because they told me. They were certain I had paired them deliberately, because their stories were so similar.

I hadn't. I didn't know most of the people in the room, and definitely not them.

I have thought about their response ever since. People are so hungry for an excuse to build a connection. Given a structure that asks them to tell their story and to listen — really listen — they find each other across distances that had seemed, five minutes earlier, unbridgeable. There were real differences in their experiences. What they took away was a new sense of solidarity. It was, they told me, the first time they had ever done anything like that with a colleague — never mind with the students they taught.

Every time I use that exercise, the response is the same. The room fills with something I can only describe as relief. I have more photographs on my phone of auditoriums full of teachers breaking into pairs — smiling, leaning toward each other, bridging — than of almost anything else in my professional life. What the exercise does is not complicated. It creates the conditions Allport described: equal status, a common purpose, a structure that makes genuine cooperation possible. It takes about ten minutes to set up. It asks almost nothing of the institution. And it produces, reliably, the thing that 94% of our students say they have never experienced in school — the sense that someone in the room wants to know who they are.

* * *

What is missing from most schools is not content. It is not good intentions. It is a holistic vision of what schools actually are. We tend to think of schools as places that teach things — and curriculum matters. But schools are engines of socialization as much as instruction. The rituals that mark the school day, the interactions in the hallway, the unspoken rules about whose language is welcomed and whose is corrected, who is greeted by name and who is watched with suspicion — these teach as surely as any lesson plan. And without a sense of belonging, the academic mission fails on its own terms. The research is unambiguous: students who feel unseen, unwelcome, or unsafe do not learn as well. Belonging is not the soft side of schooling. It is the foundation.

Belonging, as the research demands we define it, is not a feeling. It is a condition. It is the experience of being valued for who you are — your full identity, your language, your family's story — while being genuinely invited into participation in shared life. A student belongs when the school sees what she brings and builds from it, rather than asking her to leave it at the door.

The distinction matters because feelings can be manufactured. You can put up a welcome sign. You can celebrate heritage months. You can declare that everyone belongs. But if the curriculum still erases students' histories, if the assessment still measures only what they lack, if the adults in the building still don't know how to talk about the differences in the room — the sign on the wall is a lie, and the students know it.

The girl in the tenement knew it before she could name it. The young man in London had been waiting years for a classroom that made space for him. The visitors who came in complaining about the neighborhood knew it, too, though they pointed it out in the wrong direction. The conditions that made those encounters work — the real artifacts, the right questions, the adult who didn't rush to the answer, the exercise that asked people to simply listen — were not accidental. They were built.

* * *

There is a painful irony in how schools manage their attention. They are not, in fact, passive institutions. They are intensely reactive — to the next educational trend, the next mandated assessment, the next technology promising transformation. What they are rarely reactive to is what actually matters: the dynamics of the community outside the school doors, the identities, backgrounds, and experiences of the students in the seats, the perspectives of the parents who send them, the civic challenges their neighborhoods are navigating. When those identities do get noticed — when test scores reveal opportunity gaps, and someone needs an explanation — they are too often treated as the problem rather than the starting point. The student's language, their family's immigration story, their cultural background: evidence of deficit, not sources of strength.

And so when something ruptures — a bullying incident, a taunt in the hallway, a slur on a locker — schools shift into crisis response. An assembly is called. A speaker is brought in. A statement is issued. The moment passes. Nothing structural changes. And the next incident produces the same cycle, because the conditions that made it possible were never addressed — only the eruption.

This is not education. It is damage control. And it communicates something to students: difference is a problem that erupts periodically and must be managed, rather than a permanent condition that requires ongoing capacity and genuine curiosity.

The infrastructure model starts from a different premise. It asks: what would this school need to have in place so that when the crisis comes — and it will come — the school already has the relationships, the practices, the shared language to respond?

It looks like educators who know their students' stories. Not as data points but as human narratives. Who knows which students are carrying the weight of a parent's deportation hearing? Which students are navigating between two languages and two cultures? Which students are afraid to say where their family is from? This is Moll and González's funds of knowledge made daily practice — not a research project but a habit of attention.

It looks like a curriculum that activates what students bring rather than bypassing it. Not by putting people on display — no student should feel like a representative of their culture, called on to explain their family's story to a room full of curious strangers. But by creating opportunities for safe sharing and building moments for respectful curiosity about the similarities and differences in experience and perspective, learning becomes reciprocal. When a history class studying immigration draws on the actual immigration experiences in the room, student voices become the text, as much as any text. The classroom becomes what Dewey imagined — a place where democracy is practiced, not just described — when teachers stop listening for right or wrong answers and start listening for thinking, reflection, and wonderings. Project Zero's See-Think-Wonder routine captures this beautifully: the shift from interrogation to inquiry, from extracting information to genuinely not knowing what a student will say next, and being glad for it.

It looks like professional development that treats teachers as the intellectuals they are. Not training sessions where someone tells them what to do, but sustained communities of practice where educators develop the judgment to read their own communities and respond.

Sandy Mendoza is one of those educators. A first-generation Mexican-American who started kindergarten in the United States without speaking English, Sandy carries her own experience of being a newcomer into everything she does. She started an International Café — a space for recently arrived students to connect through shared stories and struggles. After a workshop where she heard about the importance of making diversity visible, she brought the idea back to her students. They ran with it. They decided to greet classmates each morning in the languages and representing the nationalities actually present in their school — welcoming bus riders with music and signs in Spanish, Arabic, Dari, and more. The choice was deliberate: not a generic celebration of diversity in the abstract, but a specific recognition of the people who were actually there. A fifth grader said, "Wow, this is the best morning of my life." The newcomers — students who had felt invisible — felt, in Sandy's words, like rockstars. No one scripted that project. Sandy built the conditions and shared an idea. Her students made it their own.

My sister-in-law teaches English to adult learners in Pomona, California. Her mandate is language instruction. What she has built is a culture of belonging so strong that her students regularly take charge of creating celebrations that reinforce community — bringing in food from Mexico, Thailand, the Middle East, Central and South America, turning a language classroom into a space where the traditions people carry are offered as gifts. No one assigned this. The conditions in her classroom made it possible.

My wife, also named Sandy — Sandra Margarita Anastasia Smith-Garcés, though in these pages she is simply Sandy Smith-Garcés — leads tours for ESL and SLIFE students at the Museum of Fine Arts in Boston. Before each visit, she learns about the students' backgrounds and ensures the tour includes art from their communities. She speaks fluent Spanish, but she intentionally asks Spanish-speaking students to help her improve her vocabulary when they look at an object together — flipping the script, turning students into teachers, signaling that what they carry is expertise. This is what Allport's equal status looks like in practice: not a policy but a gesture, repeated until it becomes a culture.

These are educators doing this work in museums, in ELL classrooms, in schools, in after-school programs — proof that the conditions can be built, that belonging is not theoretical, that the work is already happening in places no policymaker has thought to look. The task is to find it, name it, and make it visible — and where it doesn't yet exist, to build it.

* * *

What all of these educators share is something that cannot be packaged and sold: they know their communities. They know who is in the room. They know which questions will open something up and which will shut it down. They have done the slow, unglamorous work of building relationships before the crisis arrives.

This is where I learned something about scale that contradicts almost everything the philanthropic world believes.

The conventional wisdom says: find what works, standardize it, scale it. Package your approach, sell it to districts, train their teachers, measure fidelity. This logic has dominated education reform for forty years, and it has produced, at scale, precisely the thin, decontextualized instruction this book has been criticizing. You cannot standardize what makes the Tenement Museum work. You cannot package the moment when a ten-year-old looks at a photograph and suddenly understands something about her own life that no one has ever explained to her. You cannot replicate the roar of a room full of teachers finally being asked to listen to each other.

What I have learned is that what works is not a product. It is a relationship between a vision and a community. The vision provides the architecture — the research base, the conceptual tools, the shared language. The community provides the knowledge —

the understanding of who lives here, what they carry, where the fault lines and the bridges are. Neither is sufficient without the other.

This means investing in local capacity through multiyear initiatives and grant support — in educators and community leaders who already have the knowledge their context requires, who need the research base, the network, and the shared language, but do not need anyone to tell them who their students are. It means longer time horizons, more tolerance for ambiguity, and a willingness to fund the conditions for impact rather than demanding that every dollar produce a measurable return on a timeline that bears no relationship to the pace of human change. The indicators exist — educator retention, educator self-efficacy, the quality of relationships across difference, whether students show up and stay, and whether families trust the institution enough to walk through the door. They are slower and harder to capture than a test score. They are also the ones that tell you whether anything real is happening.

It means giving the tools away. Not selling them to districts as packages. Not gating them behind contracts. Giving them away, because the scale of the need dwarfs any business model, and because the premise of the work is that the knowledge belongs to the communities that use it.

* * *

The presence of a trusted adult — someone a young person can name, someone who knows their story, someone who signals that they belong — is one of the strongest predictors of academic persistence, emotional resilience, and civic engagement that developmental researchers have identified. It is not a nice-to-have. It is the load-bearing relationship on which everything else rests.

Flipping the Suárez-Orozco findings in reverse: ninety-four percent of the students who most need a trusted adult feel they have no one. We have never treated relationship-building as infrastructure. This is the gap. Not a content gap, not a curriculum gap, but a relationship gap — the failure to build the most basic condition that Allport identified. Institutional support begins here: an adult who sees you, who knows your story, who signals that what you carry is welcome in this room.

Closing that gap is not a program. It is a reorientation of what schools understand themselves to be for. And it starts with the same thing the Tenement Museum started with, the same thing that young man in London was asking for, the same thing those two teachers in Boston discovered when they were finally given ten minutes and a question and permission to listen: the conviction that the encounter, handled with intention, changes people. That the questions students bring — even the ones that surprise you, especially the ones that surprise you — are not interruptions to the curriculum. They are the curriculum.

FIELD NOTE II

"Content is no longer scarce. The web saw to that. What is scarce is the capacity to curate it responsibly."

I run a national organization that argues, in essence, that the work must be local. I have never fully resolved the tension in that sentence. I'm not sure it can be resolved. What follows is my attempt to be honest about what living inside it actually looks like.

You cannot build a belonging ecosystem from a distance, and you cannot sustain one without support — the steering committee that keeps the work visible, the professional learning community where educators process what happened in class on Tuesday, the administrator who makes room in the schedule and defends the work when it comes under pressure, the district coordinator who connects teachers across schools so no one is doing it alone.

The framework travels. The application cannot. The teacher in Lewiston who has built relationships with Somali families over a decade knows things about that community that I will never know from Cambridge. The educator in El Paso who walks her students past the border wall every morning carries a knowledge that no curriculum guide can contain.

And yet those educators need something that their local context cannot provide on its own. They need the research — the evidence that what they are doing is grounded, not just well-intentioned. They need the network — the connection to others doing similar work in different places, the reassurance that they are not alone. They need the language — a shared vocabulary for what they are building, precise enough to be useful and flexible enough to fit their context.

I saw this tension play out in a conversation I have thought about many times since. We were discussing how to help teachers find and use online resources — whether to link out to content on other sites, to curate broadly, to treat the web as a commons. A colleague raised a concern I understood immediately: external links would take users off our platform, and our metrics tracked engagement on our own site. It was a reasonable institutional concern. It was also, I realized, a sign that something had shifted. We had built something real and now we were protecting it — and the protection was starting to shape the decisions.

A similar moment came in a conversation about evaluation design. For me, fidelity meant something specific: were educators using our guiding questions, engaging students in the kinds of moral reasoning the approach demanded? But others around the table pushed toward a different definition — which specific resources were teachers actually using, how many, how often? It was a perfectly reasonable thing to want to measure. But I kept thinking: we had confused the tactic with the goal. The resource was supposed to serve the reasoning. Now the resource was becoming the thing we were measured by.

What I carried away from both conversations was not frustration with my colleagues — they were responding to real pressures that any organization faces as it grows. What I carried away was a question my mother had wrestled with her whole career: how do you build something durable without letting the institution become more important than the purpose it was built to serve?

But it is what the work actually requires. The hunger I described in the first field note — the hunger for purpose, for the deeper work — is matched by a hunger for the capacity to do it well. Teachers don't want to be told what to teach about difference. They want to be equipped to figure it out for themselves, with their students, in their communities.

The fidelity-versus-responsiveness tension never resolves. It just gets managed, day by day, community by community, by people doing the hardest work in education with the least structural support.

PART III

The Demands

THE STAKES

"The retreat from civic education produces a civic vacuum. And vacuums get filled."

Everything I have described so far — the encounter as a permanent condition, the history of betrayal, the science of contact, the retreat from civic purpose, the tradition that shows us what to build, the glimpses of what is possible — all of it leads here. To the question that should keep us awake: what happens if we don't?

But also: what becomes possible if we do?

***

There is a causal chain, and it is not speculative. It is visible. It is happening now.

When schools retreat from civic education — when they narrow their purpose to test scores and workforce readiness, when they treat the encounter with difference as someone else's problem — they leave a generation without the dispositions that democratic life requires. Not without information. Any AI can explain how a bill becomes a law. What no technology can do is sit across from someone whose experience contradicts your own and remain in the conversation. What no algorithm can build is the habit of seeing those unlike yourself as legitimate participants in shared life rather than threats to it.

The retreat from civic education produces a civic vacuum. And vacuums get filled.

What fills the vacuum is the encounter without Q — the unstructured, unsupported meeting with difference that the research tells us goes badly. Demographic change continues. Proximity increases. The world arrives through screens, through migration, through the inescapable interconnection of modern life. And young people navigate all of it with whatever narratives they have absorbed — from families, from media, from algorithms optimized to exploit their fears.

The result is what Richeson's research predicts: when demographic change is framed as a threat, it produces threat responses. When the story people carry is one of loss — of a country being taken from them, of an identity under siege, of strangers who do not belong — the encounter with difference confirms the story.

Research on authoritarian populism across the developed world identifies a consistent pattern: hostility toward immigrants is the strongest predictor of support for anti-democratic movements. Not economic anxiety alone. Not cultural conservatism alone. It is the specific conviction that outsiders threaten the nation's identity that opens the door to leaders who promise to protect that identity by any means necessary.

The means turn out to require dismantling democratic norms. Restricting the press. Demonizing the courts. Attacking the legitimacy of elections. Concentrating power. The leader who begins by promising to protect "real Americans" from foreign contamination ends by attacking the institutions that protect all Americans from tyranny.

The civic education that might have inoculated against this — that might have built the dispositions to resist demagogues, to evaluate claims critically, to see pluralism as strength rather than threat — was the education that was defunded, marginalized, and abandoned over the past fifty years.

* * *

What makes this moment different from previous cycles of nativist backlash is that the erosion is not only in attitudes. It is in capacities. The dispositions that democratic life requires — the ability to hold complexity, to tolerate ambiguity, to distinguish between disagreement and enmity, to maintain relationships across difference — these are not natural endowments. They are built through practice, through education, through the kind of structured encounter that Allport described and that schools have largely stopped providing.

You cannot fix this by teaching people the law alone. The crisis is not ignorance of democratic procedures. It is the erosion of democratic dispositions — the habits of mind and heart that make people want to sustain democratic life even when it is difficult, even when it requires sharing power with those they fear or dislike or do not understand.

Learned Hand understood this in 1944, standing before newly naturalized citizens in Central Park: "I often wonder whether we do not rest our hopes too much upon constitutions, upon laws and upon courts. These are false hopes; believe me, these are false hopes. Liberty lies in the hearts of men and women; when it dies there, no constitution, no law, no court can even do much to help it."

What lives in the hearts — or fails to — is specific. It is the belief that pluralism is a strength, not a threat. That every person possesses inalienable rights regardless of where they were born, what language they speak, or what god they pray to. That my rights do not carry more weight than my neighbor's. That disagreement is not betrayal. That sharing power with those unlike me is not losing something but building something.

* * *

But I said at the beginning of this chapter that the question is not only what happens if we don't. It is what becomes possible if we do. And this is where I need to return to a basic foundation of this book: Encounter is not the problem. Encounter is the engine.

Every significant cultural achievement in human history has emerged from encounter. The Renaissance was not produced by a homogeneous society. It was produced by the collision of Greek, Roman, Arabic, and Christian traditions in Italy's trading cities. Jazz was not produced by one tradition. It was produced by the encounter between African musical traditions, European harmonic structures, and the specific conditions of Black life in America. The scientific revolution was not the product of one culture working in isolation.

Immigration does not drain a society. It fuels it. The evidence is overwhelming: immigrants start businesses at higher rates than native-born people. They file patents at higher rates. They win Nobel Prizes at higher rates. They found companies that define the modern economy.

And the encounter itself — the friction, the dissonance, the creative tension that comes from navigating difference — is not a cost to be minimized. It is the engine of growth. Research on diverse teams consistently shows that they outperform homogeneous teams on complex problems — not because they are more comfortable, but because they are less comfortable, and that discomfort forces better thinking.

The students in our classrooms carry this potential. The child who speaks three languages is not a problem to be remediated. She is an asset so extraordinary that any rational society would invest in cultivating her. The family that carries knowledge of two continents, two legal systems, two ways of organizing community life — they are not a burden. They are a resource that a society genuinely committed to its own flourishing would race to activate.

The stakes, then, are not only what we lose if we fail. They are what we gain if we succeed.

We gain a generation that can hold the conversation we are currently failing to have — the conversation about who we are, who belongs, what we owe each other, and how we build shared life across genuine difference. We gain young people who can resist demagogues, not because they have been taught to recognize propaganda, but because they carry within them the experience of productive encounter — the lived knowledge that those unlike them are not threats but partners in the shared project of democratic life.

We gain the flashes. The insights that come only from the frontier. The culture, the innovation, the art, the ideas that no homogeneous society has ever produced and no homogeneous society ever will.

FIELD NOTE III

"The conditions Gordon Allport identified are not luxuries for peaceful times. They are the infrastructure that holds when everything else is being torn apart."

I need to be clear about what we have not solved. It's what keeps me up at night and driven during the day.

The political environment is more hostile to this work than at any point in my career. The very language of belonging and inclusion has been weaponized. In some states, laws have been passed that restrict what teachers can say about race, about history, about identity. In others, immigration enforcement has entered school zones — the one place that was supposed to be safe. Families are afraid. Educators are afraid. The civic infrastructure this book describes is under direct assault.

In January 2025, the federal government revoked the long-standing "sensitive locations" policy that had kept immigration enforcement away from schools, churches, and hospitals. Schools were no longer off limits. What followed was not theoretical. It was violent, chaotic, and targeted.

In Chicago, ICE agents operated in force around schools in Albany Park and Little Village. At a Logan Square elementary school, students were at recess when they were rushed inside after an agent threw tear gas at a car near the playground. Teachers created sanctuary teams, posted Know Your Rights cards in their classrooms, and tracked detention cases involving their students' parents. Gabriel Paez, a teacher working with recently arrived immigrant students on the Northwest Side, said what every educator in this book has been saying: "If you are not physically safe, if you feel like you are in jeopardy or your family is unsafe, we know that higher-level thinking will not develop as it should in children." Hundreds of students from Little Village Lawndale High School staged a walkout after back-to-back raids in their neighborhood, marching down 26th Street carrying signs and blowing whistles. Illinois eventually passed the Safe Schools for All Act, which prohibits schools from disclosing students' immigration status.

In Los Angeles, ICE agents twice attempted to enter LAUSD elementary schools, claiming they were conducting "wellness checks" — a lie, as two U.S. senators later confirmed. Building leaders denied them entry both times. A fifteen-year-old boy with disabilities was handcuffed at gunpoint outside Arleta High School in a case of mistaken identity. Parents were afraid to attend their children's graduation ceremonies. Superintendent Alberto Carvalho deployed over 1,000 staff members and volunteers to patrol streets around more than 100 schools, reroute bus lines, and establish a compassion fund for families in hiding. "In our community," Carvalho said, "there are no sidewalks for immigrants and separate sidewalks for everybody else. Everybody walks the same journey to school and everybody then walks back home."

And then Minneapolis. In December 2025, the Department of Homeland Security launched Operation Metro Surge — which it called the largest immigration enforcement operation ever conducted — sending more than 2,000 agents into the Twin Cities. Federal agents followed school buses. They detained a five-year-old boy, Liam Conejo Ramos, as he walked home from school with his father. They detained a ten-year-old girl on her way to school. ICE agents killed two civilians — Renée Good, a mother who had just dropped her six-year-old at school, and Alex Pretti, a nurse who was filming agents outside a donut shop. At one suburban school, more than fifty students did not return after winter break.

The community's response was extraordinary. Parents and neighbors organized patrols around elementary schools, using walkie-talkies, Signal group chats, and whistles to warn families and staff of enforcement activity. Teachers delivered groceries, water, diapers, and schoolwork to families afraid to leave their homes. Fifty thousand people marched through the streets on the coldest day of the year. One educator, standing in the crowd with a sign, said, "When I first started teaching, we had fire drills and tornado drills. Then we started to have to develop safety drills in case of an active shooter in the school or neighborhood. Now, we have to develop safety protocols in case our own government shows up to hurt or kidnap our students."

* * *

The current assault on immigrant communities has taught us something important: schools alone cannot build belonging. They never could. Urie Bronfenbrenner understood this half a century ago. His ecological systems theory showed that a child's development is not shaped by any single setting but by nested systems — the microsystem of family and classroom, the mesosystem of connections between home and school and community, the exosystem of policies and institutions that shape conditions from a distance, the macrosystem of cultural values and laws that set the terms for all of it.

This means that belonging cannot be built solely from the school outward. It requires both. When ICE agents wait outside the school, it does not matter how welcoming the classroom is — the exosystem has overwhelmed the microsystem. The ecology has to hold at every level.

What Chicago, Los Angeles, and Minneapolis showed us is that the infrastructure holds when it has been built at every level of the ecology. The teacher who knows which families are at risk. The principal who knows the law and refuses to open the door. The neighbors who organize patrols. The students who walk out because their parents cannot. The superintendent who reroutes the buses. The mayor who signs an executive order. The governor who passes a law. That is Bronfenbrenner's ecology in action — micro to macro, every layer reinforcing the others, every layer necessary.

The current assault is not an argument against the work described in this book. It is the most urgent argument for it.

I do not know that we will succeed. But I know we have to try. We understand how people encounter and respond to difference. We understand what education can do when it is designed with intention. We understand the conditions that make encounters across difference build community rather than fragment it. The struggle is not new, and it will not end. But Camus was right — we must imagine Sisyphus happy. The boulder does not defeat him. The pushing is the point. The need has never been greater. The knowledge has never been clearer. The people who do this work have never been more ready. I could not keep pushing without the people around me.

A theme of this book is the importance of relationships — the argument that belonging is built not through programs but through the connections among people who see one another and hold one another accountable to a shared purpose. I am incredibly fortunate in my own. I am surrounded by a strong team at Re-Imagining Migration, a wise board, and remarkable individual and organizational partners and collaborators whose work inspires and challenges me every day.

So I will end this field note with a plea as much as an invitation: cultivate the relationships within and across your ecosystem. Find the people doing this work in your community, in your district, in your state, in your field. Hold onto them. Build with them.

WHAT THIS ASKS OF US

"The plate is not too full. The plate is organized around the wrong meal."

The purpose is this: education in a pluralistic society must be organized around the encounter. Not as one goal among many but as the animating mission around which everything else takes shape. The question every school should ask — the question that should drive curriculum, assessment, professional development, community partnerships, everything — is: are we building the conditions under which our students learn to navigate difference with understanding rather than fear?

This is not a new purpose. It is the original purpose, reconstructed — stripped of the assimilationist betrayal, grounded in research, informed by the liberatory educational tradition, made honest by reckoning with what went wrong.

* * *

The demographic reality makes this argument urgent, not theoretical. By 2045, the United States will have no racial or ethnic majority. Among children under eighteen, that milestone has already passed. One in four students in American schools today has at least one immigrant parent. In the largest districts, it is closer to one in two. The foreign-born population has more than quadrupled since 1970. Communities that were homogeneous a generation ago are being remade — not temporarily, not reversibly, but permanently.

And unlike the great waves of immigration at the turn of the twentieth century, today's newcomers are everywhere. They are in suburbs and exurbs, in rural communities and gateway cities, in places that have never before experienced significant immigration — in the meatpacking towns of Kansas and Nebraska, in the agricultural valleys of eastern Washington, in the poultry-processing communities of the Deep South, in the dairy country of rural Wisconsin. In many rural communities, newcomers are not displacing existing residents — they are the reason the community still exists. Without them, schools would close. Hospitals would close.

We have been here before. The Great Migration — when six million Black Americans moved from the rural South to the cities of the North, Midwest, and West between 1910 and 1970 — was one of the largest internal migrations in American history. It was also one of the most generative. The encounter between Southern Black traditions and Northern urban life unleashed an explosion of cultural, musical, political, and economic innovation that reshaped the nation. The Harlem Renaissance. The Chicago blues. The Detroit sound. None of this emerged from homogeneity. All of it emerged from encounter.

My grandparents lived through this encounter. They ran a grocery store on the South Side of Chicago that served migrants straight off the trains that brought them north. For my father, growing up in that store, getting to know the customers and the neighborhoods they came from, opened a world beyond his own Jewish South Side community. Among the customers he remembered was Mamie Till, the mother of Emmett Till, who was brutally murdered by white supremacists when he traveled south from Chicago to Money, Mississippi, to visit his family. The South Side was a place where Jewish immigrants and Black migrants built lives alongside one another — not without tension, not without the hierarchies that structured American life, but with a proximity that made abstraction impossible.

* * *

That proximity — the kind that makes abstraction impossible, that forces you to see the person rather than the category — is what schools are positioned to build. Not accidentally, the way my father encountered it growing up behind a counter on Maxwell Street. Intentionally. As a matter of design.

This book is not a call for one more reform initiative. It is a call for a different understanding of what schools are for.

The plate is not too full. The plate is organized around the wrong meal. Reorganizing it — making the encounter the animating purpose, the thing everything else serves — produces a different kind of education entirely.

In this education, literacy is not a decontextualized skill. It is the capacity to read the world — Freire's insight, made daily practice. In this education, history is not a set of facts to be memorized. It is a discipline of moral reasoning — a way of understanding how the choices of ordinary people, under pressure, produced the world we inhabit and might produce a different one. In this education, the arts are not a frill. They are the space where encounter becomes tangible — where students create together across difference and discover what collaboration makes possible.

The Architecture of a Belonging Standard

I have described what this work asks of educators, leaders, policymakers, funders, and families. But the work does not belong to any one of them. It belongs to all of them — together, in relationship, across the ecology that Bronfenbrenner described. What is missing is the connective tissue — a shared commitment that links every layer of the ecology around a common understanding of what belonging requires and how to build it. Not a curriculum. Not a program. A standard is not a curriculum. It is a declaration — the way a community says publicly and accountably that it has decided belonging is too important to leave to individual goodwill.

I have long admired what David Lubell built when he founded Welcoming America — an organization that, under his leadership and now Rachel Péric's, works with local governments and community organizations across the country to create policies and practices that foster inclusion of immigrants and all residents. The Welcoming Standard showed that it was possible to move from aspiration to infrastructure, from good intentions to shared accountability, at the community level.

At a Welcoming America gathering in Dallas, David, Fernande Raine, and I started talking about what it would look like to create something analogous for schools. Fernande co-leads History Co:Lab, an organization that brings together historians, educators, and communities to use historical thinking as a tool for civic engagement. That conversation was the genesis of an idea we are still developing.

What follows is not a blueprint. It is a set of possibilities meant to inspire, not prescribe. The full architecture of a belonging standard will require the kind of collaborative design that this book argues for: built by communities, grounded in local knowledge, responsive to the people it is meant to serve. It will require input from community leaders, time set aside for educators to lead the process, openness to critique, and willingness to take action.

* * *

Mapping Bridges and Barriers. Before a community can build a sense of belonging, it must understand its own landscape honestly — which means mapping not only where the work is already happening but where it is being resisted. Where are the places where people from different backgrounds already meet as equals — the soccer league, the community garden, the after-school program, the workplace where cooperation is structured into the daily routine? These are bridges. They exist in every community, often unrecognized and unsupported — the educator who started a space for newcomers, the teacher who flips the script and lets students become the experts, the museum guide who builds the tour around who is actually in the room. But the map is incomplete without the barriers: the parent who complained and won, the administrator who quietly killed a program to avoid conflict, the community member who attended every school board meeting until the work was defunded, the educator who burned out doing this alone and left. Resistance is not an aberration. It is a predictable feature of this work, and a belonging standard has to account for it. Understanding where the resistance comes from — what fears it expresses, whose interests it protects, what it would take to move it — is as important as celebrating what is already working. A community that maps only its bridges will be surprised every time a barrier appears. A community that maps both is prepared.

* * *

Listening at 360 Degrees. I carry a dream shaped by the work of Kevin Jennings, who understood the power of asking the right questions of the right people before almost anyone else did. When Kevin founded GLSEN in 1990, one of the most important things the organization built was the National School Climate Survey — a tool that asked LGBTQ youth directly about their experiences in schools. What the survey surfaced was devastating: the pervasive harassment, the silence of adults, the systematic failure of schools to protect queer students. But the survey did more than document the crisis. It identified what made the difference. Schools that had Gay-Straight Alliances reported lower rates of harassment. Schools where educators had received professional development on LGBTQ issues were safer. The data pointed not just to the problem but to the architecture of the solution.

The dream is this: what if we listened to everyone in the educational ecosystem?

Students know whether the classroom is a place where they can bring their whole selves — or whether parts of them must be left at the door. They know whether the curriculum has ever reflected anyone who looks like them, speaks like them, or comes from where they come from. They know whether the adults in the building see them as assets or problems.

And yet students, for all they carry, can only see from where they stand. Teachers, parents, administrators, and the rest of the school community see something different.

Teachers know whether they have the preparation and the institutional support to do this work — or whether they are improvising alone, without time, without resources, without anyone above them who understands what they are trying to do. They know which students are struggling in ways the data never captures, and which families have stopped showing up because the school never made them feel welcome in the first place. Parents know whether the school communicates with them in their language — not just literally, but culturally. Whether the events assume a particular kind of family. Whether their knowledge of their own children is ever treated as expertise. Administrators know where the pressure comes from and what it costs to push back. They know which teachers are doing this work quietly and which ones have burned out trying. Other school staff — the counselors, the custodians, the cafeteria workers, the bus drivers

— often know things about students that no teacher ever learns, because they inhabit different spaces in the school day and students trust them differently. Some of the most powerful acts of kindness toward newcomer students I have heard about have come from custodial staff and cafeteria workers — many of whom are immigrants themselves and recognize something in a child eating alone or standing lost in a hallway that no job description has prepared them to see. They greet kids in their home language. They make sure they get lunch. They check in. They notice. They are doing belonging work every day without anyone ever calling it that, without any training or institutional support — because they remember what it felt like to arrive somewhere that wasn't sure it wanted them.

Each of these people sees the ecology from a different vantage point. Each carries knowledge that the others lack. And none of them is ever asked all of it, systematically, in a way that connects what they see to what everyone else sees.

Many schools are already surveying students about belonging — and that instinct is right. But the questions are too rarely framed in ways that speak to the diverse experiences and expectations of the students being asked. The instruments are not culturally responsive. They were not designed with immigrant-origin students in mind, with families navigating between two languages and two worlds, with young people whose relationship to belonging is shaped by forces the survey never asks about. And when the data comes back, it is almost always disaggregated by race — a useful lens but an incomplete one. It misses the experiences of first and second generation immigrant students entirely, flattening their stories into categories that don't capture what they are actually living.

This matters because the research is detailed on this point: immigrant-origin students report their sense of belonging decreasing the longer they are in American schools. That finding should be an alarm. But if the survey instrument doesn't ask the right questions — if it can't distinguish between a student who arrived last year and a student whose grandparents were born here, if it can't hear the difference between a student who feels invisible and one who feels actively erased — then the alarm never sounds.

The kind of listening this work requires is harder than administering a survey. It asks schools to design instruments that are responsive to their actual communities — that include questions shaped by the knowledge of the families and educators who live and work there. It asks for disaggregation that goes beyond race to include generation, language background, and immigration experience. And it asks for follow-through: not just collecting the data but returning to the communities that generated it, asking what it means, and letting the answer drive what changes.

Put it all together — what students experience, what teachers notice, what parents feel when they walk through the door, what administrators know about where the pressure comes from and where the bright spots are, what the custodian has observed in a child who eats alone every day — and you would have something schools almost never have: an honest picture of the ecology. Not a snapshot of test scores, not a satisfaction survey, but a genuine map of what is working, what isn't, and where the energy needs to go.

That is what the data should be for.

* * *

Preparing Educators for the World That Exists. Any serious effort to build belonging will eventually run into the same discovery: the educators asked to do this work were never prepared for it. Teacher preparation programs in the United States were largely designed for a country that no longer exists.

The educators who do this work well — and there are many of them — learned it despite their preparation, not because of it. They should not have had to build it themselves.

We cannot ask schools to build what their teachers were never taught to construct. A belonging standard, a community mapping process, a 360-degree listening effort — all of these create a demand for educators prepared to work within them. That demand must eventually reshape how we recruit, prepare, and support teachers.

* * *

I have offered three possibilities — mapping, listening, preparation — not as a complete architecture but as gestures toward what could be built. They share a common logic: each starts from the community rather than from an external prescription. Each trusts that the people closest to the experience carry knowledge that no outside expert can replace. Each makes the ecology visible. And each insists that belonging is not a feeling to be cultivated but a condition to be constructed.

A community belonging standard may never be finished in the way a curriculum or a policy is finished. It is, by its nature, a living commitment — one that must be renewed and adapted as communities change, as new families arrive, as the encounter continues to reshape the places where we live and learn together.

Welcoming America offers a model worth studying. The national Welcoming Standard did not begin as a national standard. It began as local practice — communities doing the work, documenting what they found, articulating what belonging required in their specific contexts. Over time, those local articulations were convened, compared, and refined into a framework that other communities could engage with — not as a mandate but as a mirror.

Something similar is possible for schools. A convening of local actors who have led belonging work in their own communities — who have done the audits, built the teams, navigated the resistance, and learned what the standard actually requires in practice — could articulate a national framework grounded in that accumulated experience. Communities could then engage that framework on their own terms: using it as a self-assessment tool, seeking peer review against it, or pursuing recognition of their commitment. The standard that emerges from this process carries its own accountability, because the people who built it can see whether it is being honored or ignored. The document is not the standard. The process that produced it is.

The educators closest to this work are already telling us what the standard requires. When you ask them to look honestly at their schools — to audit what is actually present rather than what is intended — a consistent picture emerges across contexts as different as a therapeutic day school in a major northeastern city and a rural high school on a remote Hawaiian island. Physical access is almost never the primary barrier. Doors are open. What is not open, consistently, is the experience of being genuinely welcomed. The language gap is structural, not incidental — most schools were built for a different population than the one they now serve. And belonging, where it exists at all, depends almost entirely on specific individuals rather than institutional design: the one teacher who checks in, the one counselor who arranged a buddy, the one administrator who knows a student's name. When that person leaves, the belonging leaves with them. This is not a curriculum problem. It is not a professional development problem. It is not a policy problem. It is an infrastructure problem — and the difference matters, because infrastructure is what we build when we decide that something is too important to leave to individual goodwill.

Martha Minow, the groundbreaking legal scholar who has spent decades thinking about education, justice, and democracy — and who read an early draft of this manuscript — pointed me toward a body of research that names what I had been observing without quite knowing what to call it. Positive deviance — a term coined by researchers Jerry and Monique Sternin, initially working in public health — rests on a deceptively simple premise: in any community facing a difficult problem, there are already individuals who have found a way through, using the same resources and facing the same constraints as everyone else. The question is not how to import a solution from outside but how to find the people who are already solving the problem and learn from what they are doing.

Those people are already in our schools. Sandy M. didn't wait for a curriculum. The custodian who greets kids in their home language didn't wait for a professional development session. The teacher who knows which students are carrying the weight of a parent's deportation hearing developed that knowledge through attention, not through training. Positive deviance research suggests that the most powerful thing an institution can do is not design a new program but create the conditions for existing solutions to spread — to make visible what is already working, name it, and build from it.

The scale of the challenge requires a movement, not a brand. It requires people who will never encounter the organization I helped build, who will never read this book, who will develop their own approaches and push beyond anything we have imagined. It requires a shared sense of purpose that crosses organizational boundaries and ideological lines — the recognition that preparing young people for lives of encounter is not a progressive agenda or a conservative agenda but a democratic necessity.

What I am asking is that we begin. Not together in any organized sense — there is no membership, no headquarters, no single program to adopt. Patrice O'Neill, the founder of Not In Our Town, explains that the people she spoke to in Minneapolis said their movement to push back against Operation Metro Surge was not leaderless but leaderful, many people leading from where they stood, without waiting for permission or coordination from above. That is what I am hoping for here — that we work from a shared recognition that the encounter is the condition, that belonging is the infrastructure, and that the work of building both is the most important thing schools can do.

Those who have always known this are already doing it, in classrooms and community centers and museum galleries and professional development rooms across the country — and in your community, right now, whether you know it yet or not. The first task is to find them. Lift up what they are doing. Learn from it. Ask what it would take to make it durable, to build the conditions that survive a single teacher's departure or a change in leadership or a shift in the political wind.

Then look honestly at the gaps. What is working, and for whom? What isn't, and why? Where are the students who still have no adult in the building who sees them? Where are the educators who are hungry to do this work but have never been given the permission or the preparation? Where are the communities that don't yet know they need this, or have been told they don't deserve it?

This means administrators must protect the space — not just tolerate this work when it is convenient, but defend it when it isn't, schedule time for it, and make clear to their communities that belonging is not an add-on but a core commitment. It means community members must show up for school board meetings, for budget conversations, for the moments when the work comes under attack, and for the quieter moments when an educator doing this work needs to know that someone outside the building sees what they are doing and values it.

It means philanthropists must fund what doesn't photograph well — the professional learning community that meets every Tuesday, the coordinator who holds the network together, the fellowship that takes three years to change how an educator sees their work, the unrestricted operating support that lets an organization respond to what its community actually needs rather than what last year's grant required it to do. And it means asking a different question at the end of a grant cycle — not "did this program succeed?" but "what does this community now have that it didn't have before?" The answer will look different depending on the work. For organizations doing direct service, it may mean families who received support they could not have found elsewhere. For organizations trying to build a field, change a norm, or shift a practice, it means asking whether the community now owns something that will outlast the grant — whether the relationships outlast the initiative, whether the coordinator who holds it together was hired from the community rather than imported from outside it, whether what began as a funded project has become simply how things are done here. Both matter. The mistake is applying the logic of field-building to direct service, or the logic of direct service to field-building. Funders who conflate the two end up measuring the wrong things in both directions.

That is the work. It belongs to everyone who decides to take it up — the educator who stays, the administrator who protects the space, the funder who invests before the market exists, the student who stands in front of a room of adults and teaches them something they couldn't have learned any other way.

The conditions that make this moment so difficult are the same conditions that make this moment so important. The encounter is not going away. The children are already here. The question that has organized this entire book — whether we will prepare them to navigate difference with understanding rather than fear — is not a question about the future. It is a question about what we are willing to do right now, today, in the schools and communities we actually inhabit.

My mother's school failed her. That failure was not inevitable. Neither is ours.

WHAT COMES NEXT

A lot of you are going to ask me what now. I know this because I have spent years with educators, school leaders, foundation officers, and policymakers who have heard some version of this argument and then, almost before I have finished, leaned forward and said: you have done a good job explaining what's wrong, but what should I actually do?

The argument I have tried to make is that belonging is not a program to be adopted but a condition to be built — and that the building looks different in every community, every school, every room. A protocol that works in a rural Idaho middle school experiencing demographic change for the first time will not land the same way in a Boston high school where fourteen languages are spoken in the hallways. The questions that open a conversation in one place will close it in another. The leader who can carry this work in one district would struggle in the next one.

What I can tell you is that the people who know how to do this in your community almost certainly already exist. They are in your schools, your community organizations, your parent groups

— doing the work quietly, without institutional recognition, waiting to be found and taken seriously. The first task is not to import a solution. It is to look honestly at what is already present, and ask what it would take to make it durable.

For educators: this asks you to see your students as a whole. Not as test scores, not as English proficiency levels, not as behavior problems or success stories, but as human beings carrying histories, languages, knowledge, and wounds that are the raw material of education. It asks you to know your community — to understand who lives there, what they carry, where the fault lines and the bridges are. It asks you to treat the encounter with difference not as a disruption to your lesson plan but as the lesson itself.

This is harder than teaching to a test. It requires the kind of professional judgment that the accountability movement — sometimes deliberately, sometimes as an unintended consequence — spent forty years eroding. It requires being an intellectual, not a technician. It requires courage, because doing this work well means entering territory that is uncomfortable, contested, and politically charged.

But I have seen it happen hundreds of times: what happens when educators are trusted with this work. They rise to it. The hunger is there. What has been missing is the permission, the preparation, and the institutional support.

For students: this asks more of you than most adults will admit. You already know whether your school sees you. You know which hallways feel safe and which don't, which classrooms make space for who you are and which ask you to leave part of yourself at the door. That knowledge is not incidental to the work of building belonging — it is the foundation of it.

Students are not the beneficiaries of a belonging standard. They are its most essential architects. A mapping process that doesn't center student voice is not a map — it is a guess. A standard built without students is a standard built about them, which is precisely the error this book has been arguing against from the first page.

Some of the most powerful belonging work I have witnessed has been led by students themselves. But nothing has stopped me in my tracks quite like immigrant-origin youth who have taken professional development into their own hands — designing and leading PD for their own teachers about the experiences and needs of immigrant youth. Not as spokespersons. Not as props in someone else's lesson. As practitioners. They study their audience, develop their content, and stand in front of the adults in their school and say: here is what you need to understand, and here is what we need from you.

The educators in those rooms are not passive. Their job is to make it possible — to create the opportunity, offer coaching, and show up not as experts but as the audience the students are trying to reach. That reversal is not a gimmick. It is Allport's equal status, made real. It is funds of knowledge, activated. It is the encounter the book has been describing, happening in the room where learning is supposed to happen.

The adults in this book — the educators, the leaders, the funders, the policymakers — are necessary. They are not sufficient. The question is whether they will create enough space for students to lead, and whether they will have the humility to follow.

For school leaders: this asks you to protect the space — and to prioritize the work, not merely permit it. The principal who says "keep going" when a parent complains about a classroom conversation on immigration is doing more for democratic education than any policy document. The superintendent who makes belonging an organizing principle rather than an add-on is changing the conditions under which every teacher in the district operates.

This is not soft work. The research is clear: students who feel seen, safe, and connected learn more. Belonging is not the alternative to academic achievement. It is the precondition for it. The district leader who invests in belonging infrastructure is making an academic bet — and it is one of the safest bets in education.

And while we are here: there are educators doing this work every day whose contribution is almost entirely invisible. English Language and Multilingual Learner teachers are among the most skilled community builders in any school — they know their students' families, they navigate between languages and cultures, they build the bridges between newcomer families and the institution that no one else has thought to build. They are often treated as specialists at the margins of the school's real work. Many of them are, in fact, often doing the work this book describes better than almost anyone — not because it was assigned to them, but because their students' survival in the school depended on it. School leaders who want to build belonging infrastructure should start by asking their EL and MLL teachers what they already know — and then making that knowledge visible to the rest of the staff.

For policymakers: this asks you to rethink what schools are for and how policy supports that purpose. The narrowing of education over the past fifty years was not inevitable — it was driven by policy choices that imported a business logic into an enterprise that is fundamentally local, fundamentally relational, fundamentally human. Standards matter. Testing has a place within a larger portfolio of how we understand what schools accomplish. But when test scores become the sole measure of success, they crowd out everything they cannot capture.

We need policies that recognize education as a civic enterprise, not only an economic one. Schools are not factories producing workers. They are the places where young people learn whether the society they live in has a place for them — and whether they have the capacity to help build it.

A growing number of states are experimenting with broader school quality indices that include climate, belonging, and civic measures alongside academic ones — moving from a single test score to a dashboard that asks whether students feel safe, whether families trust the institution, whether the school is preparing young people for democratic life and not just the workforce. That is the lever worth pushing. Accountability structures shape what schools understand themselves to be for. Change what you measure and you begin to change what schools do.

For funders: this asks you to invest differently. The philanthropic world has spent decades funding individual organizations with their own theories of change, asking each to prove that it alone can solve the problem. The problem is too large and too complex for any single organization. What is needed is investment in infrastructure — in the connective tissue between organizations, in the local capacity that persists after the grant cycle ends, in the slow, unglamorous work of building systems rather than launching initiatives.

The social enterprise movement has done real good — it has pushed nonprofits to think harder about sustainability, efficiency, and the value they actually deliver. But it has also imported assumptions that don't always hold in education.

The first is that demand precedes supply. In most markets, it does. In education reform, often it doesn't. The most important work happens before the market exists — before communities know they need it, before policymakers have language for it, before the norm has been established that makes the demand legible. Nonprofits are the research and development arm of the education sector. They take risks that most districts won't — and in the best cases, they do this in genuine partnership with districts, building the proof of concept together rather than delivering it from outside. Fee-for-service models and earned income strategies have their place — but applied too early, or too broadly, they force organizations to follow demand rather than shape it. The foundation's role is precisely to fund the work before it's demanded — to invest in norm-shaping, not just norm-following.

At Re-Imagining Migration, we were asked to demonstrate market demand at the very moment we were seeking support to develop the tools that would allow educators to pilot the work in the first place. You cannot prove demand for something that doesn't yet exist. Education nonprofits working on the frontier of practice deserve the same faith as digital entrepreneurs, who are routinely capitalized to develop innovations that haven't found their form in the market yet. Not blind faith — accountability matters, and evidence should accumulate — but faith that comes before the market, not after it.

The communities that most need belonging infrastructure are rarely the ones who can pay for it. An organization that prices its way to sustainability prices out the people it exists to serve. Philanthropic investment in this space is not a bridge to a market. It is the point.

The second assumption is about scale. What you want is not scale. What you want is growth — and growth is something different. Growth is what happens when seeds are planted in the soil and develop according to the conditions they find. Local adapters — not local adopters — are the right unit of change. A field that can only count what is easy to count will keep funding what is easy to count. The indicators for growth exist — educator retention, the quality of relationships across difference, whether families trust the institution enough to walk through the door, whether students show up and stay. They are slower and harder to capture than a test score. But they are the ones that tell you whether anything real is happening.

The third assumption is about visibility. Organizations doing this work are not politically neutral in the eyes of those who feel threatened by the vision they represent. The work can be distorted, weaponized, and turned into a political football. This happened to Facing History and Ourselves when my mother led it. A program cited as exemplary by the Department of Education was attacked, defunded, and caricatured — not because it was partisan, but because it was clear. Clarity, in a polarized environment, reads as provocation to those who prefer the fog. An organization that calibrates its content to the loudest objection in every room will eventually stand for nothing. Stay focused on what you are actually trying to do, and let the noise be noise.

For families: this asks you to want more. More than test scores. More than college admissions. More than the narrow version of success that the system has trained you to demand. It asks you to want for your children what you would want for the world they will inherit: the capacity to live among those unlike themselves with understanding, with curiosity, with the civic courage that democratic life requires.

For those who want concrete tools and approaches, Re-Imagining Migration is a good place to start — it's where I spend my time when I'm not writing books.

A NOTE TO MY MOTHER

Mom, as I wrote this book, I learned something about our family that I think would have made you smile — and then made you furious that no one taught it to you.

You know the story we carried. Eastern European Jews. The shtetl. The pogroms. The steerage class voyage to America. Ancestry's genetic analysis confirmed what we always assumed: 99% Ashkenazi Jewish. As if that settled it. As if that described a people rooted in one place, one tradition, one story.

But it turns out that category contains multitudes.

Dad always said his family had ancient roots along the trade routes — connections that went back long before Eastern Europe. He had even run his DNA with scientific colleagues before he passed — he had the proof, at least for his side of the family. But without documentation we could share, the story remained another Terry Strom legend to the rest of us.

So I took the Ancestry data and ran a deeper analysis — moving beyond the autosomal DNA that shuffles and recombines every generation and into the haplogroups that never change, the genetic fossils that trace direct paternal and maternal lines back thousands of years. What I found vindicated him — and then surprised me further. My paternal haplogroup, G-M377, has deep roots in the Punjab and the Indus Valley, confirming what Dad already knew. But my maternal haplogroup, M33c, is a rare South Asian branch as well. The permanent signatures — the markers that survive unchanged across millennia — place our deepest ancestors on both sides not only in the shtetls of Eastern Europe but along the ancient trade routes between South Asia and the Mediterranean.

Dad knew his half of the story. He just couldn't have known that your side carried it too.

Our ancestors were almost certainly connected to the Radhanites — Jewish merchants who operated along the Silk Road and the spice routes, who were the dominant international traders of their era. Active from the eighth to the tenth centuries, they served as essential intermediaries between the Christian and Islamic worlds at a time when those civilizations were closed to one another's merchants. They spoke Arabic, Persian, Greek, French, Spanish, and Slavic. They traded silk, spices, and perfumes from the Rhône Valley to the coast of China. A ninth-century Persian geographer described them journeying "from west to east, from east to west, partly on land, partly by sea."

They were people of encounter. People who made their living — and their meaning — at the frontier between civilizations. People for whom the meeting with difference was not a problem to be managed, but the very basis of their existence.

The 99% Ashkenazi is the story of the last thousand years — a community that turned inward, often because the world forced it to do so. But the deeper story, the one written in the DNA that doesn't change, is a story of movement across continents, of encounter across civilizations, of people who thrived precisely because they could navigate difference.

I expect you would have loved this, Mom. Dad's story probably wouldn't have been a suprise. But yours? That's the twist neither of us saw coming. It turns out the encounter with difference wasn't just something you devoted your life to. It was written into you, on both sides, long before any of us had words for it.

You built Facing History because your school in Memphis failed to help you understand the world you were already living in. You knew, even then, what was missing. And now it turns out the story goes back further than either of us imagined. Back along the Silk Road. Back through centuries of encounter. Back to people who understood that the frontier is not a place of danger to be avoided, but the place where everything important happens.

You should not have had to build it yourself. That is what schools are for.

We owe the young people in our care nothing less.

Notes on Sources

This book draws on research from multiple fields — social psychology, education, sociology, neuroscience, history, and political science — as well as on three decades of practice as an educator and organizational leader. It is a work of synthesis, not scholarship in the traditional sense. I have tried to make the argument read like a story rather than an academic text, which means I have not interrupted the prose with footnotes or endnotes. But the claims I make rest on the work of researchers and thinkers whose contributions deserve to be traceable, and on readers who want to go deeper, who deserve a path.

What follows is organized by chapter. Where I have quoted directly, I have identified the source and, where possible, the page number. Where I have drawn on a body of research rather than a single study, I have tried to point the reader to the work that most directly shaped my thinking.

Educational resources developed at Facing History and Ourselves and Re-Imagining Migration have reached millions of students in tens of thousands of classrooms worldwide, including books, lessons, and films on immigration, civil and human rights, genocide, and prejudice. The Moving Stories exercise described in Chapter 6 was developed in collaboration with Carola Suárez-Orozco. The student survey data on belonging, home language use, and assimilation pressure draws on YouthTruth, Immigration Initiative at Harvard, *YouthTruth and Re-Imagining Migration Student Survey 2023–24* (YouthTruth, 2024), as well as unpublished findings from the 2025 class of Re-Imagining Migration fellows.

I owe a particular debt to the scholars whose work forms the intellectual foundation of this book: Gordon Allport, Thomas Pettigrew, and Linda Tropp on intergroup contact; John Dewey and Paulo Freire on democratic education; Gloria Ladson-Billings,

Django Paris, Luis Moll, Norma González, and Verónica Boix Mansilla on culturally sustaining and globally responsive pedagogy; Claude Steele, Gregory Walton, and Carol Goodenow on belonging and academic performance; Zaretta Hammond on neuroscience and culture; Urie Bronfenbrenner on ecological systems; Franz Boas on the cultural construction of emotional response; Lawrence Kohlberg and Carol Gilligan on moral development; John Rogers on civic education in conditions of political stress; Kwame Anthony Appiah on the ethics of identity; Martha Minow on law, equality, and the institutional design of pluralism; and Carola Suárez-Orozco and Marcelo Suárez-Orozco on the experiences of immigrant-origin students.

I owe a particular and personal debt to Margot Stern Strom — my mother and the founder of Facing History and Ourselves — whose claim that democracy is a work in progress, shaped by the choices ordinary people make, runs through every chapter of this book. See Margot Stern Strom, "A Work in Progress," in *Working to Make a Difference: The Personal and Pedagogical Stories of Holocaust Educators Across the Globe*, ed. Samuel Totten (Lanham, MD: Lexington Books, 2003).

The Boas material in Chapter 3 draws on Noga Arikha's essay "Who Am I When I Care? Emotion Through the Lens of Franz Boas," *Aeon*, March 2026, and on Boas's own "Psychological Problems in Anthropology" (1910). The concept of "patterned practices" as culturally transmitted emotional habits is developed in Arikha's recent biography, *Franz Boas: In Praise of Open Minds* (2025).

Errors of fact or interpretation are mine.

Four books form the intellectual foundation of this argument and deserve to be named at the outset. John Dewey's *Democracy and Education* (1916) was the original inspiration — the conviction that democratic life is not preparation for education but education itself, practiced in the encounters of shared life. Gordon Allport's *The Nature of Prejudice* (1954) provided the research architecture: the demonstration that contact across difference, under the right conditions, transforms how human beings see one another. Rucker Johnson's *Children of the Dream* (2019) showed what that architecture looks like when it is actually built — and what it costs when it is dismantled. And Carola Suárez-Orozco, Marcelo Suárez-Orozco, and Irina Todorova's *Learning a New Land* (2008) grounded the abstract argument in the concrete experience of the young people this book is ultimately about. Everything else builds from these four.

Behind these four sits Kwame Anthony Appiah's *The Ethics of Identity* (Princeton: Princeton University Press, 2005), whose account of how human selves are formed through encounter — rather than through retreat into bounded identity — provides the philosophical foundation for the pedagogy this book describes. The argument that schools must be designed for encounter rests, finally, on Appiah's claim that identity is not what we protect but what we make in relation to others.

Below are specific references and notes by chapter.

Introduction

Lillian Smith, *Killers of the Dream* (New York: W.W. Norton, 1949; revised 1961).

Chapter 1: The Encounter Is the Condition

U.S. Census Bureau population projections. See "Projections of the Size and Composition of the U.S. Population: 2014 to 2060" and updated 2023 projections.

On the majority-minority under-18 population: U.S. Census Bureau, 2020 Census results.

One in four students with at least one immigrant parent: Migration Policy Institute, "Children in U.S. Immigrant Families," MPI Data Hub, tabulation of U.S. Census Bureau 2024 American Community Survey data, updated 2025. Available at migrationpolicy.org/programs/data-hub/charts/children-immigrant-families.

See also National Academies of Sciences, Engineering, and Medicine, *The Integration of Immigrants into American Society* (Washington, DC: National Academies Press, 2015).

The foreign-born population has quadrupled since 1970, according to U.S. Census Bureau historical data.

The Diversity Index figures are from the U.S. Census Bureau, "Racial and Ethnic Diversity in the United States: 2010 Census and 2020 Census," August 2021.

Chapter 2: The Dream and Its Betrayal

On the Freedmen's Bureau and the post-Emancipation hunger for schooling, see Eric Foner, *Reconstruction: America's Unfinished Revolution, 1863–1877* (New York: Harper & Row, 1988); and W.E.B. Du Bois, *Black Reconstruction in America* (1935; reprint, New York: Free Press, 1998).

Booker T. Washington on the hunger for education: Booker T. Washington, *Up From Slavery* (New York: Doubleday, 1901).

Charlotte Forten diary: Charlotte Forten Grimké, *The Journals of Charlotte Forten Grimké*, ed. Brenda Stevenson (New York: Oxford University Press, 1988).

Frederick Douglass on literacy: Frederick Douglass, *Narrative of the Life of Frederick Douglass, an American Slave* (Boston: Anti-Slavery Office, 1845).

Horace Mann and the common school: Horace Mann, *Annual Reports to the Massachusetts Board of Education* (various years, 1837–1848).

Captain Richard Henry Pratt, "The Advantages of Mingling Indians with Whites": Address at the Nineteenth Annual Conference of Charities and Correction, Denver, 1892. Reprinted in Richard Henry Pratt, *Battlefield and Classroom: Four Decades with the American Indian, 1867–1904*, ed. Robert M. Utley (New Haven: Yale University Press, 1964).

Interior Department investigation: U.S. Department of the Interior, *Federal Indian Boarding School Initiative Investigative Report* (Washington, DC: Bureau of Indian Affairs, May 2022).

Reyna Grande: Reyna Grande, *The Distance Between Us: A Memoir* (New York: Atria Books, 2012).

Angela Valenzuela on subtractive schooling: Angela Valenzuela, *Subtractive Schooling: U.S.-Mexican Youth and the Politics of Caring* (Albany: SUNY Press, 1999).

Mary Antin, *The Promised Land* (Boston: Houghton Mifflin, 1912).

On Dewey as a thinker carried forward into contemporary civic education: see John Rogers and the IDEA team's work at UCLA, discussed in the Chapter 9 notes below.

James Baldwin, *Collected Essays* (New York: Library of America, 1998), pp. 678–686.

Chapter 3: What Happens When We Meet

Robert D. Putnam, "E Pluribus Unum: Diversity and Community in the Twenty-First Century," *Scandinavian Political Studies* 30, no. 2 (2007): 137–174.

Ryan D. Enos, "Causal effect of intergroup contact on exclusionary attitudes," *Proceedings of the National Academy of Sciences* 111, no. 10 (2014): 3699–3704.

Jens Rydgren and Patrick Ruth, "Voting for the Radical Right in Swedish Municipalities: Social Marginality and Ethnic Competition?" *Scandinavian Political Studies* 34, no. 3 (2011): 202–225.

On the parallel "halo effect" in France — radical-right support concentrated not where immigrants live but in the homogeneous areas surrounding them — see Gilles Ivaldi and Jocelyn Evans, "Contextual Effects of Immigrant Presence on Populist Radical Right Support: Testing the 'Halo Effect' on Front National Voting in France," *Comparative Political Studies* 54, no. 5 (2021): 823–854.

Marco Gießelmann, David Brady, and Tabea Naujoks, "The Increase in Refugees to Germany and Exclusionary Beliefs and Behaviors," *American Journal of Sociology* 130, no. 3 (2024): 725–763.

Maureen A. Craig and Jennifer A. Richeson, "On the Precipice of a 'Majority-Minority' America: Perceived Status Threat From the Racial Demographic Shift Affects White Americans' Political Ideology," *Psychological Science* 25, no. 6 (2014): 1189–1197.

Gordon W. Allport, *The Nature of Prejudice* (Cambridge, MA: Addison-Wesley, 1954).

Thomas F. Pettigrew and Linda R. Tropp, "A Meta-Analytic Test of Intergroup Contact Theory," *Journal of Personality and Social Psychology* 90, no. 5 (2006): 751–783.

Linda R. Tropp and Suchi Saxena, "Re-Weaving the Social Fabric through Integrated Schools: How Intergroup Contact Prepares Youth to Thrive in a Multiracial Society," research brief, National Coalition on School Diversity (2018). See also Linda R. Tropp, ed., *Making Diversity Work* (Washington, DC: American Psychological Association, 2020).

Franz Boas on "patterned practices" and the cultural construction of emotional response: Noga Arikha, "Who Am I When I Care? Emotion Through the Lens of Franz Boas," *Aeon*, March 2026, available at aeon.co/essays/who-am-i-when-i-care-emotion-through-the-lens-of-franz-boas. See also Noga Arikha, *Franz Boas: In Praise of Open Minds* (New Haven: Yale University Press, 2025), and Franz Boas, "Psychological Problems in Anthropology," *American Journal of Psychology* 21, no. 3 (1910): 371–384.

Fatima Mernissi, *Scheherazade Goes West: Different Cultures, Different Harems* (New York: Washington Square Press, 2001).

The formulation $X = (R \times 1/D) \div Q$ is my own synthesis. It draws on Allport's contact conditions; Pettigrew and Tropp's meta-analytic confirmation; Ryan Enos's experimental demonstration that proximity without structured interaction increases hostility; Jennifer Richeson's research on how framing shapes whether diversity is experienced as threat or opportunity; and Gießelmann, Brady, and Naujoks's finding that national anxiety about refugees coexisted with decreased concern in districts where refugees actually settled.

Chapter 4: How We Failed to Build It

Rucker C. Johnson, *Children of the Dream: Why School Integration Works* (New York: Basic Books, 2019).

Brown v. Board of Education, 347 U.S. 483 (1954).

Swann v. Charlotte-Mecklenburg Board of Education, 402 U.S. 1 (1971).

Milliken v. Bradley, 418 U.S. 717 (1974). The Marshall passage quoted in this chapter is from Justice Thurgood Marshall's dissent at 418 U.S. 782.

On the legal and constitutional aftermath of *Brown* and the long shadow it casts over American education, see Martha Minow, *In Brown's Wake: Legacies of America's Educational Landmark* (New York: Oxford University Press, 2010). Minow's account of how *Brown*'s promise was narrowed in subsequent decades — and what remains possible within the constitutional frame — informs this chapter's argument about the gap between the dream and its institutional fulfillment.

On Lawrence Kohlberg and Carol Gilligan and the intellectual environment in which Facing History was founded: Lawrence Kohlberg, *The Philosophy of Moral Development: Moral Stages and the Idea of Justice* (San Francisco: Harper & Row, 1981); Carol Gilligan, *In a Different Voice: Psychological Theory and Women's Development* (Cambridge, MA: Harvard University Press, 1982).

On the federal review of Facing History and the Christina Jeffrey, Phyllis Schlafly, and Shirley Curry materials: Melinda Fine, *Habits of Mind: Struggling Over Values in America's Classrooms* (San Francisco: Jossey-Bass, 1995). For Margot Stern Strom's own account of the founding of Facing History and Ourselves and the federal review that followed, see Margot Stern Strom, "A Work in Progress," in *Working to Make a Difference: The Personal and Pedagogical Stories of Holocaust Educators Across the Globe*, ed. Samuel Totten (Lanham, MD: Lexington Books, 2003), 69–104. See also Strom and William S. Parsons, *Facing History and Ourselves: Holocaust and Human Behavior* (Watertown, MA: Intentional Educations, 1982), and the substantially revised 1994 edition of the Resource Book. Additional documentation comes from Margot Stern Strom's papers, now archived at the University of Illinois.

National Commission on Excellence in Education, *A Nation at Risk: The Imperative for Educational Reform* (Washington, DC: U.S. Department of Education, 1983).

On the effects of No Child Left Behind on curriculum narrowing: Jennifer McMurrer, "Choices, Changes, and Challenges: Curriculum and Instruction in the NCLB Era," Center on Education Policy (2007).

On the decline of civic education: Campaign for the Civic Mission of Schools, *Guardian of Democracy: The Civic Mission of Schools* (Philadelphia: Leonore Annenberg Institute for Civics, 2011). See also Peter Levine and Kei Kawashima-Ginsberg, "The Republic Is (Still) at Risk—and Civics Is Part of the Solution," Jonathan M. Tisch College of Civic Life, Tufts University, 2017.

Field Note #1

The field notes draw on my own experience and observation. No external sources are cited in Field Note #1.

Chapter 5: The Capacities We Need

John Dewey, *Democracy and Education* (New York: Macmillan, 1916).

On Dewey's relationship with Jane Addams and Anzia Yezierska: Robert B. Westbrook, *John Dewey and American Democracy* (Ithaca: Cornell University Press, 1991); Louis Menand, *The Metaphysical Club* (New York: Farrar, Straus and Giroux, 2001). On Yezierska: Louise Levitas Henriksen, *Anzia Yezierska: A Writer's Life* (New Brunswick: Rutgers University Press, 1988).

Paulo Freire, *Pedagogy of the Oppressed*, trans. Myra Bergman Ramos (New York: Continuum, 1970).

Claude M. Steele, *Whistling Vivaldi: How Stereotypes Affect Us and What We Can Do* (New York: W.W. Norton, 2010). See also Claude M. Steele and Joshua Aronson, "Stereotype threat and the intellectual test performance of African Americans," *Journal of Personality and Social Psychology* 69, no. 5 (1995): 797–811.

Rudine Sims Bishop, "Mirrors, Windows, and Sliding Glass Doors," *Perspectives: Choosing and Using Books for the Classroom* 6, no. 3 (1990).

Gloria Ladson-Billings, *The Dreamkeepers: Successful Teachers of African American Children* (San Francisco: Jossey-Bass, 1994).

See also Gloria Ladson-Billings, "Toward a Theory of Culturally Relevant Pedagogy," *American Educational Research Journal* 32, no. 3 (1995): 465–491.

Django Paris, "Culturally Sustaining Pedagogy: A Needed Change in Stance, Terminology, and Practice," *Educational Researcher* 41, no. 3 (2012): 93–97. See also Django Paris and H. Samy Alim, eds., *Culturally Sustaining Pedagogies: Teaching and Learning for Justice in a Changing World* (New York: Teachers College Press, 2017).

Luis C. Moll, Cathy Amanti, Deborah Neff, and Norma González, "Funds of Knowledge for Teaching: Using a Qualitative Approach to Connect Homes and Classrooms," *Theory into Practice* 31, no. 2 (1992): 132–141. See also Norma González, Luis C. Moll, and Cathy Amanti, eds., *Funds of Knowledge: Theorizing Practices in Households, Communities, and Classrooms* (Mahwah, NJ: Lawrence Erlbaum, 2005).

Gholdy Muhammad, *Cultivating Genius: An Equity Framework for Culturally and Historically Responsive Literacy* (New York: Scholastic, 2020).

Zaretta Hammond, *Culturally Responsive Teaching and the Brain* (Thousand Oaks, CA: Corwin, 2015).

On the cultivation of perspective-taking, interdisciplinary thinking, and the dispositions required to navigate difference in classrooms shaped by global migration: Verónica Boix Mansilla and Anthony Jackson, *Educating for Global Competence: Preparing Our Youth to Engage the World* (New York: Asia Society / Council of Chief State School Officers, 2011). See also Verónica Boix Mansilla, "Interdisciplinary Learning," in *The Oxford Handbook of Interdisciplinarity*, 2nd ed. (Oxford: Oxford University Press, 2017), and Verónica Boix Mansilla and Devon Wilson, "What is Global Competence, and What Might it Look Like in Chinese Schools?" *Journal of Research in International Education* 19, no. 1 (2020): 3–22.

Carol Goodenow, "Classroom Belonging Among Early Adolescent Students: Relationships to Motivation and Achievement," *Journal of Early Adolescence* 13, no. 1 (1993): 21–43.

Gregory M. Walton and Geoffrey L. Cohen, "A Brief Social-Belonging Intervention Improves Academic and Health Outcomes of Minority Students," *Science* 331, no. 6023 (2011): 1447–1451. See also Shannon T. Brady, Geoffrey L. Cohen, Shoshana N. Jarvis, and Gregory M. Walton, "A Brief Social-Belonging Intervention in College Improves Adult Outcomes for Black Americans," *Science Advances* 6, no. 18 (2020): https://www.science.org/doi/10.1126/sciadv.aay3689.

Angela Valenzuela, *Subtractive Schooling: U.S.-Mexican Youth and the Politics of Caring* (Albany: SUNY Press, 1999).

Carola Suárez-Orozco, Marcelo M. Suárez-Orozco, and Irina Todorova, *Learning a New Land: Immigrant Students in American Society* (Cambridge, MA: Harvard University Press, 2008).

Chapter 6: What This Looks Like

Jacob A. Riis, *How the Other Half Lives: Studies Among the Tenements of New York* (New York: Charles Scribner's Sons, 1890).

Sarfraz Manzoor, *Luton, Actually* (short film, 2007). See also Sarfraz Manzoor, *Greetings from Bury Park* (London: Bloomsbury, 2007).

Suárez-Orozco, Suárez-Orozco, and Todorova, *Learning a New Land* (see Chapter 5 citation). The 6% and 3% findings — and the corresponding 94% figure cited later in this chapter — are from this longitudinal study of more than 400 newly arrived immigrant students across twenty public schools in Boston, Cambridge, and the San Francisco Bay Area, conducted over five years beginning in 1997.

Sandy Mendoza: Adam Strom, interview with Sandy Mendoza, Re-Imagining Migration, 2022. Available at reimaginingmigration.org.

Project Zero See-Think-Wonder thinking routine: Project Zero, Harvard Graduate School of Education, available at pz.harvard.edu/thinking-routines. The application of Project Zero's thinking routines to globally diverse classrooms — and the framing of difference as a generative condition for inquiry — is developed at length in Verónica Boix Mansilla and Anthony Jackson,

Educating for Global Competence: Preparing Our Youth to Engage the World (Asia Society / CCSSO, 2011).

Field Note #2

Field Note #2 draws on my own experience and observation. No external sources are cited.

Chapter 7: The Stakes

Kwame Anthony Appiah, *The Ethics of Identity* (Princeton: Princeton University Press, 2005), is the philosophical foundation for this chapter's argument that pluralism is not a threat to identity but the condition of its formation. Appiah's account of identity as relational — constituted in encounter rather than secured against it — underwrites the case made throughout this book for schools as civic infrastructure. See also Kwame Anthony Appiah, *Cosmopolitanism: Ethics in a World of Strangers* (New York: W.W. Norton, 2006).

On the contested question of how schools should respond to cultural and religious difference — including the headscarf debates in France and the broader question of what equality means when communities hold different beliefs about appropriate practices — see Martha Minow, Richard A. Shweder, and Hazel Rose Markus, eds., *Just Schools: Pursuing Equality in Societies of Difference* (New York: Russell Sage Foundation, 2008). Minow's chapter, "We're All for Equality in U.S. School Reforms: But What Does It Mean?," examines how American schools navigate the tension between formal equality and substantive recognition of difference. See also the volume's predecessor, Richard A. Shweder, Martha Minow, and Hazel Rose Markus, eds., *Engaging Cultural Differences: The Multicultural Challenge in Liberal Democracies* (New York: Russell Sage Foundation, 2002).

On authoritarian populism and anti-immigrant attitudes: Yascha Mounk, *The People vs. Democracy: Why Our Freedom Is in Danger and How to Save It* (Cambridge, MA: Harvard University Press, 2018). See also Steven Levitsky and Daniel Ziblatt, *How Democracies Die* (New York: Crown, 2018), and Ruth Ben-Ghiat,

Strongmen: Mussolini to the Present (New York: W.W. Norton, 2020).

Learned Hand, "The Spirit of Liberty" (address at "I Am an American Day," Central Park, New York City, May 21, 1944). Reprinted in Learned Hand, *The Spirit of Liberty: Papers and Addresses of Learned Hand*, ed. Irving Dillard (New York: Alfred A. Knopf, 1952).

On diverse teams outperforming homogeneous teams: Scott E. Page, *The Diversity Bonus: How Great Teams Pay Off in the Knowledge Economy* (Princeton: Princeton University Press, 2017).

On immigrants and innovation: National Academies of Sciences, Engineering, and Medicine, *The Economic and Fiscal Consequences of Immigration* (Washington, DC: National Academies Press, 2016).

On the relationship between anti-immigrant attitudes and support for authoritarian movements — the empirical case for the "strongest predictor" framing in this chapter: Pippa Norris and Ronald Inglehart, *Cultural Backlash: Trump, Brexit, and Authoritarian Populism* (Cambridge: Cambridge University Press, 2019). See also Cas Mudde and Cristóbal Rovira Kaltwasser, *Populism: A Very Short Introduction* (Oxford: Oxford University Press, 2017).

On civic dispositions and democratic character: Danielle Allen, *Talking to Strangers: Anxieties of Citizenship since Brown v. Board of Education* (Chicago: University of Chicago Press, 2004). See also Timothy Snyder, *On Tyranny: Twenty Lessons from the Twentieth Century* (New York: Tim Duggan Books, 2017).

The Camus reference is to Albert Camus, *The Myth of Sisyphus and Other Essays*, trans. Justin O'Brien (New York: Vintage, 1955; orig. published in French, 1942).

Field Note #3

The conditions in this Field Note are documented at scale in John Rogers et al., *The Fear is Everywhere: U.S. High School Principals Report Widespread Effects of Immigration Enforcement* (Los Angeles: UCLA's Institute for Democracy, Education, and Access, 2025). The Rogers IDEA studies, taken together — *Teaching and*

Learning in the Age of Trump: Increasing Stress and Hostility in America's High Schools (UCLA IDEA, 2017); *School and Society in the Age of Trump* (Rogers, J., Ishimoto, M., Kwako, A., Berryman, A., Diera, C., UCLA IDEA, 2019), available at idea.gseis.ucla.edu/publications/school-and-society-in-age-of-trump; and *The Fear is Everywhere* (2025) — provide the systematic national context for what the field accounts in Chicago, Los Angeles, and Minneapolis describe locally.

Department of Homeland Security, "Enforcement Actions in or Near Protected Areas," memorandum from Acting Secretary Benjamine Huffman to ICE and CBP, January 20, 2025. This memorandum rescinded Alejandro Mayorkas's October 27, 2021 memorandum, "Guidelines for Enforcement Actions in or Near Protected Areas."

Urie Bronfenbrenner, *The Ecology of Human Development: Experiments by Nature and Design* (Cambridge, MA: Harvard University Press, 1979).

Chicago: ICE tear gas near Funston Elementary School, Logan Square, October 3, 2025: Laura Rodríguez Presa, Jake Sheridan, and Tess Kenny, "Chicagoans Say ICE Agents Responded to Heckling with Tear Gas near School on Busy Northwest Side Street," *Chicago Tribune*, October 3, 2025.

Gabriel Paez quotes: Aydali Campa, "'It Is My Responsibility': Chicago Educators Try to Allay Students' Immigration Enforcement Fears," *Borderless Magazine*, November 20, 2025. Republished by *Chalkbeat Chicago*, November 24, 2025.

Little Village Lawndale High School walkout, October 28, 2025: Kate Perez, "Students Walk Out of Little Village Schools, Hold March in Protest of Recent ICE Activity," *Chicago Tribune*, October 28, 2025.

Safe Schools for All Act, Illinois: Illinois House Bill 3247 (Public Act 104-0288), signed by Governor JB Pritzker on August 15, 2025, effective January 1, 2026.

Los Angeles: ICE attempting to enter LAUSD elementary schools, April 7, 2025: "ICE Agents Denied Entry into LAUSD Elementary Schools," *K-12 Dive*, April 14, 2025.

"Wellness checks" confirmed false by senators: Senators Alex Padilla and Adam Schiff letter to HSI Acting Executive Associate Director Robert Hammer, April 18, 2025.

Arleta High School incident, August 11, 2025: "Teen with Disabilities Detained by Federal Agents at Gunpoint in Arleta," *NBC Los Angeles*, August 13, 2025.

Alberto Carvalho quotes and LAUSD actions: LAUSD press conference, August 11–13, 2025.

Minneapolis: Operation Metro Surge: "2,000 Federal Agents Sent to Minneapolis Area to Carry Out 'Largest Immigration Operation Ever,' ICE Says," *PBS News/AP*, January 6, 2026.

Liam Conejo Ramos detained, January 20, 2026: "5-Year-Old Liam Conejo Ramos Taken by ICE in Minnesota," *CNN*, January 22, 2026.

Meg Smaker, "Renee Good, Poet and Mother of 3, Was Supporting Neighbors When ICE Shot Her, Wife Says," *Minnesota Reformer*, January 9, 2026. Available at minnesotareformer.com.

Max Nesterak, "Department of Justice Opens Civil Rights Investigation into Killing of Alex Pretti," *Minnesota Reformer*, January 30, 2026. Available at minnesotareformer.com.

Luis Feliz Leon, "In the Twin Cities, a Massive Strike Against ICE," *Labor Notes*, January 2026. Available at labornotes.org/2026/01/twin-cities-massive-strike-against-ice.

Mary Ellen Flannery, "As Fear Grips Schools, Minnesota Educators Mobilize to Protect Students and Families," *NEA Today*, January 25, 2026. Available at nea.org/nea-today/all-news-articles/minnesota-educators-mobilize-protect-students-and-families.

Chapter 8: What This Asks of Us

Isabel Wilkerson, *The Warmth of Other Suns: The Epic Story of America's Great Migration* (New York: Random House, 2010).

Mamie Till and Emmett Till: Devery S. Anderson, *Emmett Till: The Murder That Shocked the World and Propelled the Civil Rights Movement* (Jackson: University Press of Mississippi, 2015).

On Welcoming America and the Welcoming Standard: welcomingamerica.org. David Lubell founded Welcoming America in

2009; Rachel Péric currently serves as the organization's Executive Director. The description of how the standard emerged from community-level work draws on conversations with David Lubell over several years.

On positive deviance: Jerry Sternin and Monique Sternin developed the positive deviance approach in public health contexts in the 1990s. For the foundational account, see Richard Pascale, Jerry Sternin, and Monique Sternin, *The Power of Positive Deviance: How Unlikely Innovators Solve the World's Toughest Problems* (Boston: Harvard Business Press, 2010). My attention to this body of research was prompted by a conversation with Martha Minow, whose *Between Vengeance and Forgiveness: Facing History after Genocide and Mass Violence* (Boston: Beacon Press, 1998) — drawn from a conference she co-led with Margot Stern Strom and dedicated to her — is the deeper source of this chapter's argument that institutions can be redesigned, after harm, in ways that hold both accountability and belonging.

The field evidence in the Belonging Standard section draws on belonging audit documentation submitted by the 2025 Belonging Fellows cohort of Re-Imagining Migration. Fellows and their schools have been anonymized.

On the positive effects of immigrant students on native-born peers: David Figlio and Umut Özek, "Unwelcome Guests? The Effects of Refugees on the Educational Outcomes of Incumbent Students," *Journal of Labor Economics* 37, no. 4 (2019): 1061–1096.

On Kevin Jennings and GLSEN: GLSEN, *The National School Climate Survey* (various years). Available at glsen.org.

To learn more about History Co:Lab, visit historycolab.org.

On Patrice O'Neill and the "leaderful" framing of community responses to violence and threat: Patrice O'Neill is the founder of Not In Our Town, which documents and supports community responses to hate violence and bias. See niot.org.

A Note to My Mother

On the Radhanites: Louis Rabinowitz, *Jewish Merchant Adventurers: A Study of the Radanites* (London: Edward Goldston, 1948). See also Shlomo Goitein, *A Mediterranean Society: The Jewish Communities of the Arab World as Portrayed in the Documents of the Cairo Geniza*, 6 vols. (Berkeley: University of California Press, 1967–1993).

The haplogroup data cited — paternal G-M377 (native to the Punjab and Indus Valley) and maternal M33c (South Asian branch) — are drawn from the author's genetic analysis via Ancestry DNA and FamilyTreeDNA, with subsequent research into the population genetics and historical literature on those lineages.

The closing line — that democracy is a work in progress, shaped by the choices ordinary people make — is hers, from Margot Stern Strom, "A Work in Progress" (cited above).

A closing note

A book like this is built from the work of others. The conversations that shaped it began long before I sat down to write and will continue after readers close it. I am grateful to the scholars whose research I have leaned on, to the educators whose practice has tested and refined the ideas here, to the students whose questions have kept the argument honest, and to the colleagues at Re-Imagining Migration and Facing History and Ourselves whose daily work makes the case for what I have only described. Whatever in this book is useful belongs to that wider community. What is wrong is mine.

www.ingramcontent.com/pod-product-compliance
Lightning Source LLC
LaVergne TN
LVHW090938150826
845672LV00006B/1548

* 9 7 9 8 9 9 5 8 3 9 8 0 4 *